Workshop on NLP and Linguistics: Finding the Common Ground 2010

(NLPLING 2010)

Held at ACL 2010

Uppsala, Sweden
16 July 2010

ISBN: 978-1-61738-819-4

Printed from e-media with permission by:

Curran Associates, Inc.
57 Morehouse Lane
Red Hook, NY 12571

Some format issues inherent in the e-media version may also appear in this print version.

Printed by Curran Associates, Inc. (2010)

For permission requests, please contact the Association for Computational Linguistics
at the address below.

Association for Computational Linguistics
209 N. Eighth Street
Stroudsburg, Pennsylvania 18360

Phone: 1-570-476-8006
Fax: 1-570-476-0860

acl@aclweb.org

Additional copies of this publication are available from:

Curran Associates, Inc.
57 Morehouse Lane
Red Hook, NY 12571 USA
Phone: 845-758-0400
Fax: 845-758-2634
Email: curran@proceedings.com
Web: www.proceedings.com

Preface

Since early 1990s, with the advancement of machine learning methods and the availability of data resources such as treebanks and parallel corpora, data-driven approaches to NLP have made significant progress. The success of such data-driven approaches has cast doubt on the relevance of linguistics to NLP. Conversely, NLP techniques are rarely used to help linguistics studies. We believe that there is room to expand the involvement of linguistics in NLP, and likewise, NLP in linguistics, and that the cross-pollination of ideas between the disciplines can greatly benefit both fields. We are pleased to present the workshop on *NLP and Linguistics: Finding the Common Ground* in order to focus on some of the work that uses NLP and linguistics for mutual benefit, and discuss future plans for continuing collaborations.

The workshop is intended to spur discussion on how NLP and linguistics can help each other, including new methods in incorporating linguistic knowledge into statistical systems to advance the state of the art of NLP, and the feasibility of using NLP techniques to acquire linguistic knowledge for a large number of languages and to assist linguistic studies. Fifteen papers were submitted and nine were accepted (one later withdrew), and the accepted papers are oriented around the following themes:

- **Research that shows awareness of a particular linguistic phenomenon and its effects on statistical systems:** Caines and Buttery discuss the zero auxiliary construction (*You talking to me?*), awareness of which can improve performance of NLP on spoken English. Samaradžić and Merlo suggest that awareness of different types of light verb constructions could affect word alignment. Su, Huang, and Chen show that the linguistic notion of evidentiality can be used for automatic detection of trustworthiness.
- **New methods in incorporating linguistic knowledge into statistical systems to improve the start of the art:** The papers by Caines and Buttery, Cook and Stevenson, Samaradžić and Merlo, and Su, Huang, and Chen all present a number of linguistic features that can be used for modeling or other corpus-based tasks.
- **Research that demonstrates the feasibility of creating NLP systems to automatically acquire linguistic knowledge for a large number of languages:** Mayer, Rohrdantz, Plank, Bak, Butt, and Keim examine a phonotactic constraint in 3,200 languages. Poornima and Good propose the repurposing of traditional word lists from historical and comparative linguistics to NLP applications.
- **Research that demonstrates the benefits of using NLP techniques to help particular linguistic studies:** This volume is rich with examples of corpus-based techniques shedding light on linguistic phenomena, including the ambiguity of German past participles (Zarrieß, Cahill, Kuhn, and Rohrer), zero auxiliary constructions (Caines and Buttery), light verbs (Samaradžić and Merlo), a paradoxical reading of "no X is too Y to Z" (Cook and Stevenson), the phonotactic constraint of Similar Place Avoidance (Mayer, Rohrdantz, Plank, Bak, Butt, and Keim), and evidentiality (Su, Huang, and Chen).
- **The realtive strengths and weaknesses of corpus-based and rule-based resources:** Plank and van Noord examine the domain portability of rule-based and corpus-trained parsers. Zarrieß, Cahill, Kunh, and Rohrer show that a corpus-based analysis can help reduce ambiguity of German past participles in a rule-based parser.

In addition to the presenters of papers, the workshop includes two panels to discuss the potential contributions of NLP to linguistics and linguistics to NLP. The panelists in the Linguistics-helps-NLP panel have been asked to address the following questions, and the questions for the NLP-helps-Linguistics panel are similar. Three panelists have written a short paper to summarize their positions, and these papers have been included in the proceedings.

1. What kinds of NLP applications could benefit from linguistics? For a particular NLP application, what is the best way of incorporating linguistic knowledge into NLP systems to improve the start of the art. (e.g., as rules in a preprocessing step, as linguistic features in a statistical system, as filters for pruning a search space, as priors in an objective function)?

2. What is the right role for a linguist in developing NLP resources (e.g., recommending features, writing rules, or building resources such as treebanks)?

3. What are the obstacles to using linguistics in NLP and how can they be removed? What do you wish you had available to you but don't?

4. How can we, as a field, encourage more collaborations between NLP researchers and linguists? Are there examples of successful collaborations, and if so, how were these facilitated?

5. What do NLP and linguistic students need to know to engage in these collaborations? How can we get students involved in collaborative research between the two disciplines?

We would like to thank everyone who made this workshop possible: ACL, the program committee, our invited speaker, the panelists, the authors, and workshop participants. Special thanks go to the US National Science Foundation for its support (NSF IIS-1027289).

Fei Xia, William Lewis, and Lori Levin

Organizers:

Fei Xia, University of Washington, USA
William Lewis, Microsoft Research, USA
Lori Levin, Carnegie Mellon University, USA

Program Committee:

Anthony Aristar, LinguistList, USA
Jason Baldridge, University of Texas at Austin, USA
Timothy Baldwin, University of Melbourne, Australia
Dorothee Beermann, NTNU, Norway
Emily M. Bender, University of Washington, USA
Steven Bird, University of Melbourne, Australia
Chris Brew, Ohio State University, USA
Michael Collins, MIT, USA
Michael Cysouw, Max Planck Institute for Evolutionary Anthropology, Germany
Hal Daume III, University of Utah, USA
Markus Dickinson, University of Indiana, USA
Alexis Dimitriadis, Utrecht Institute of Linguistics OTS, The Netherlands
Helen Aristar Dry, LinguistList, USA
Jason Eisner, Johns Hopkins Univ, USA
Erhard Hinrichs, University of Tubingen, Germany
Chu-Ren Huang, The Hong Kong Polytechnic University, Hong Kong, China
Julia Hockenmaier, UIUC, USA
Mark Johnson, Macquarie University, Australia
Kevin Knight, USC/ISI, USA
Mark Liberman, University of Pennsylvania, USA
Dekang Lin, Google, USA
Paola Merlo, University of Geneva, Switzerland
Kathy McKeown, Columbia Univ, USA
Martha Palmer, University of Colorado, USA
Dragomir Radev, University of Michigan, USA
Owen Rambow, Columbia University, USA
Dipti Misra Sharma, IIIT-H, India
Richard Sproat, Oregon Health & Science University, USA
Mark Steedman, Edinburgh, UK
Michael White, Ohio State University, USA
Richard Wicentowski, Swarthmore College, USA
Peter Wittenburg, Max Planck Institute for Psycholinguistics, The Netherlands
Andreas Witt, Institut für Deutsche Sprache, Mannheim, Germany
Nianwen Xue, Brandeis University, USA

Invited Speaker:

Steven Bird, University of Melbourne, Australia

Panelists:

Hal Daume III, University of Utah, USA
Alexis Dimitriadis, Utrecht Institute of Linguistics OTS, The Netherlands
Erhard Hinrichs, University of Tubingen, Germany
Dipti Misra Sharma, IIIT, India

Julia Hockenmaier, UIUC, USA
Eduard Hovy, USC/ISI, USA
Owen Rambow, Columbia University, USA

Sponsor:

US National Science Foundation (Grant IIS-1027289)

Table of Contents

Workshop Program

Friday, July 16, 2010

8:45–8:50 Opening Remarks

8:50–9:50 Invited Talk by Steven Bird: "The Human Language Project: Uniting computational linguistics with documentary linguistics"

Paper Session 1

9:50–10:10 *Modeling and Encoding Traditional Wordlists for Machine Applications*
Shakthi Poornima and Jeff Good

10:10–10:30 *Evidentiality for Text Trustworthiness Detection*
Su Qi, Huang Chu-Ren and Chen Kai-yun

10:30–11:00 Morning break

Panel Session 1: NLP helps Linguistics

11:00–12:00 Presentation and discussion from panelists (Hal Daume, Alexis Dimitriadis, Erhard Hinrichs, and Dipti Misra Sharma)

On the Role of NLP in Linguistics
Dipti Misra Sharma

Matching Needs and Resources: How NLP Can Help Theoretical Linguistics
Alexis Dimitriadis

Friday, July 16, 2010 (continued)

Paper Session 2

12:00–12:20 *Grammar-Driven versus Data-Driven: Which Parsing System Is More Affected by Domain Shifts?*
Barbara Plank and Gertjan van Noord

12:20–12:40 *A Cross-Lingual Induction Technique for German Adverbial Participles*
Sina Zarrieß, Aoife Cahill, Jonas Kuhn and Christian Rohrer

12:40–14:10 Lunch

Paper Session 3

14:10–14:30 *You Talking to Me? A Predictive Model for Zero Auxiliary Constructions*
Andrew Caines and Paula Buttery

14:30–14:50 *Cross-Lingual Variation of Light Verb Constructions: Using Parallel Corpora and Automatic Alignment for Linguistic Research*
Tanja Samardžić and Paola Merlo

14:50–15:10 *No Sentence Is Too Confusing To Ignore*
Paul Cook and Suzanne Stevenson

15:10–15:30 *Consonant Co-Occurrence in Stems across Languages: Automatic Analysis and Visualization of a Phonotactic Constraint*
Thomas Mayer, Christian Rohrdantz, Frans Plank, Peter Bak, Miriam Butt and Daniel A. Keim

15:30–16:00 Afternoon break

Friday, July 16, 2010 (continued)

Panel Session 2: Linguistics helps NLP

16:00–17:00 Presentation and discussion from panelists (Julia Hockenmeier, Eduard Hovy, and Owen Rambow)

Injecting Linguistics into NLP through Annotation
Eduard Hovy

17:00–17:30 Group discussion and closing

Modeling and Encoding Traditional Wordlists for Machine Applications

Shakthi Poornima
Department of Linguistics
University at Buffalo
Buffalo, NY USA
poornima@buffalo.edu

Jeff Good
Department of Linguistics
University at Buffalo
Buffalo, NY USA
jcgood@buffalo.edu

Abstract

This paper describes work being done on the modeling and encoding of a legacy resource, the traditional descriptive wordlist, in ways that make its data accessible to NLP applications. We describe an abstract model for traditional wordlist entries and then provide an instantiation of the model in RDF/XML which makes clear the relationship between our wordlist database and interlingua approaches aimed towards machine translation, and which also allows for straightforward interoperation with data from full lexicons.

1 Introduction

When looking at the relationship between NLP and linguistics, it is typical to focus on the different approaches taken with respect to issues like parsing and generation of natural language data—for example, to compare statistical NLP approaches to those involving grammar engineering. Such comparison is undoubtedly important insofar as it helps us understand how computational methods that are derived from these two lines of research can complement each other. However, one thing that the two areas of work have in common is that they tend to focus on majority languages and majority language resources. Even where this is not the case (Bender et al., 2002; Alvarez et al., 2006; Palmer et al., 2009), the resulting products still cover relatively few languages from a worldwide perspective. This is in part because such work cannot easily make use of the extensive language resources produced by descriptive linguists, the group of researchers that are most actively involved in documenting the world's entire linguistic diversity. In fact, one particular descriptive linguistic product, the wordlist—which is the focus of this paper—can be found for at least a quarter of the world's languages.

Clearly, descriptive linguistic resources can be of potential value not just to traditional linguistics, but also to computational linguistics. The difficulty, however, is that the kinds of resources produced in the course of linguistic description are typically not easily exploitable in NLP applications. Nevertheless, in the last decade or so, it has become widely recognized that the development of new digital methods for encoding language data can, in principle, not only help descriptive linguists to work more effectively but also allow them, with relatively little extra effort, to produce resources which can be straightforwardly repurposed for, among other things, NLP (Simons et al., 2004; Farrar and Lewis, 2007).

Despite this, it has proven difficult to create significant electronic descriptive resources due to the complex and specific problems inevitably associated with the conversion of legacy data. One exception to this is found in the work done in the context of the ODIN project (Xia and Lewis, 2009), a significant database of interlinear glossed text (IGT), a standard descriptive linguistic data format (Palmer et al., 2009), compiled by searching the Web for legacy instances of IGT.

This paper describes another attempt to transform an existing legacy dataset into a more readily repurposable format. Our data consists of traditional descriptive wordlists originally collected for comparative and historical linguistic research.[1] Wordlists have been widely employed as a first step towards the creation of a dictionary or as a means to quickly gather information about a language for the purposes of language comparison (especially in parts of the world where languages

[1]These wordlists were collected by Timothy Usher and Paul Whitehouse and represent an enormous effort without which the work described here would not have been possible. The RDF/XML implementations discussed in this paper will be made available at `http://lego.linguistlist.org` within the context of the Lexicon Enhancement via the GOLD Ontology project.

Proceedings of the 2010 Workshop on NLP and Linguistics: Finding the Common Ground, ACL 2010, pages 1–9,
Uppsala, Sweden, 16 July 2010.

are poorly documented). Because of this, they exist for many more languages than do full lexicons. While the lexical information that wordlists contain is quite sparse, they are relatively consistent in their structure across resources. This allows for the creation of a large-scale multilingual database consisting of rough translational equivalents which may lack precision but has coverage well-beyond what would otherwise be available.

2 The Data and Project Background

The data we are working with consists of 2,700 wordlists drawn from more than 1,500 languages (some wordlists represent dialects) and close to 500,000 forms. This is almost certainly the largest collection of wordlists in a standardized format. The average size of the individual wordlists is rather small, around 200 words, making them comparable in size to the resources found in a project like NEDO (Takenobu, 2006), though smaller than in other related projects like those discussed in section 4. While the work described here was originally conceived to support descriptive and comparative linguistics, our data model and choice of encoding technologies has had the additional effect of making these resources readily exploitable in other domains, in particular NLP. We have approached the data initially as traditional, not computational, linguists, and our first goal has been to encode the available materials not with any new information but rather to transfer the information they originally contained in a more exploitable way.

By way of introduction, the hypothetical example in (1) illustrates a traditional presentation format of a wordlist, with English as the source language and French as the target language.

(1) MAN *homme*
WOMAN *femme*

As we will describe in more detail in section 5, they key features of a wordlist entry are an index to a concept assumed to be of general provenance (e.g., MAN) and a form drawn from a specific language (e.g. *homme*) determined to be the counterpart for that concept within that language. Most typically, the elements indexing the relevant concepts are words drawn from languages of wider communication (e.g., English or Spanish).

3 Related Work in Descriptive Linguistics

Recent years have seen a fair amount of attention paid to the modeling of traditional linguistic data types, including lexicons, glossed texts, and grammars (Bell and Bird, 2000; Good, 2004; Palmer and Erk, 2007; Nordhoff, 2008). The data type of focus here, wordlists, has not seen serious treatment. Superficially, wordlists resemble lexicons and, of course, they can be considered a kind of lexical resource. However, as will be shown in section 5, there are important differences between lexicons and wordlists which have implications for how they should be modeled.

Most of the work on modeling descriptive linguistic data types has proceeded without special consideration for possible NLP applications for the data being encoded. This is largely because the work was initially a response to issues relating to the longevity of digital descriptive data which was, otherwise, quite often being encoded solely in (often proprietary) presentation formats (Bird and Simons, 2003). However, the possibility for fruitful interaction between computational linguistics and descriptive linguistics is apparent and has been the subject of some work (Palmer et al., 2009).

The work described here is also interested in this possibility. In particular, we address the question of how to model and encode a large-scale dataset that was originally intended to be used for descriptive purposes in ways that not only allow us to faithfully represent the intention of the original creator but also permit the data to be straightforwardly exploitable for new uses, including NLP. To the best of our knowledge, our work is innovative both because of the data type being explored and because the data modeling is being done parallel with the transformation of a legacy resource with significant coverage of the world's languages. This stands in contrast to most other work (again, with the exception of work done within ODIN (Xia and Lewis, 2009)) whose data, while representative, is not of the same scale.

4 Related Work on Lexicon Interoperability in NLP

The relevant related work in NLP is that focused on interoperation among lexical resources. One way to achieve this is to make use of language independent ontologies (or comparable objects) for word meanings which can serve as pivots for multilingual applications (Ide et al., 1998; Vossen, 2004; Nirenburg et al., 2004; Ronzano et al., 2010). The word senses provided by WordNet, for example, have been used for this purpose (O'Hara et al., 1998).

A recognized data modeling standard for lexical interoperation is the Lexical Markup Framework (LMF), which provides standardized framework for the description and representation of lexicons (Francopoulo et al., 2009). Instantiations of LMF have also been extended to represent WordNets, e.g., Wordnet-LMF (Soria et al., 2009), in ways which facilitate interoperation.

While we do not attempt to express the data model we develop here in LMF, doing so should be relatively straightforward. The key conceptual observation is to recognize that the sets of meaning labels found in wordlists (see section 2) can be treated either as a shared language-neutral ontology or as a kind of interlingua, both of which have already been the subject of LMF modeling (Vossen, 2004). As such, they are also comparable to language-independent ontologies of word meaning, bringing them in line with the work on multilingual NLP mentioned above.

These similarities should not be too surprising. After all, one of the functions of wordlists has been to facilitate language comparison, something which is also at the heart of multilingual NLP. An important development, however, is that new data encoding technologies can allow us to encode word list data in ways that facilitate its repurposing for NLP applications much more easily than would have been possible previously. We will come back to this in section 6.

5 Modeling Wordlists

5.1 Wordlist Entries as Defective Signs

A common linguistic conceptualization of a lexical item is to treat it as a *sign* triple: an association of a *form* with *meaning* and *grammar*. Lexical items in a lexicon generally contain information on all three aspects of this triple. Wordlists do not, and the information they encode is quite sparse. In general, they give no indication of grammatical information (e.g., part of speech), nor of language-specific semantics.

In addition, from a descriptive standpoint, lexicons and wordlists differ in the direction of the form-meaning mapping. As the example in (1) suggests, in order to create or interpret a wordlist, one begins with an abstract meaning, for example MAN, and then tries to find the word in the target language which represents the best semantic fit for that meaning. Lexicons, on the other hand, prototypically map in the opposite direction from form to meaning. Furthermore, as will be elaborated in section 5.3, the meanings employed in wordlists are not intended to refer to meanings of lexical items in specific languages. In this way, they are quite distinct from bilingual dictionaries.

We can therefore view a wordlist as a set of defective signs—containing information on the form and meaning parts of the triple, but not the grammar. The meaning information is not directly associated with the specific form but, rather, is a kind of "tag" indicating that the entire sign that a given form is associated with is the best counterpart in the language for a general concept.

Figure 1 compares the kind of information associated with signs in a lexicon to those in a wordlist. The box on the left gives a schematic form-grammar-meaning triple for the Spanish word *perro* 'dog', containing the sort of information that might be found in a simple bilingual dictionary. The box on the right schematizes the content of a parallel French wordlist entry for *chien* 'dog'. Here, no grammatical or semantic information is associated with the form, but there is an indication that in French, this lexical item is the closest counterpart to the general concept DOG. Of course, in this case, the word *chien* is not only the counterpart of DOG in French, but can be translated as *dog* in English. The semantic connection between a concept label and a lexical item may not always be so straightforward, as we will see in section 5.2.

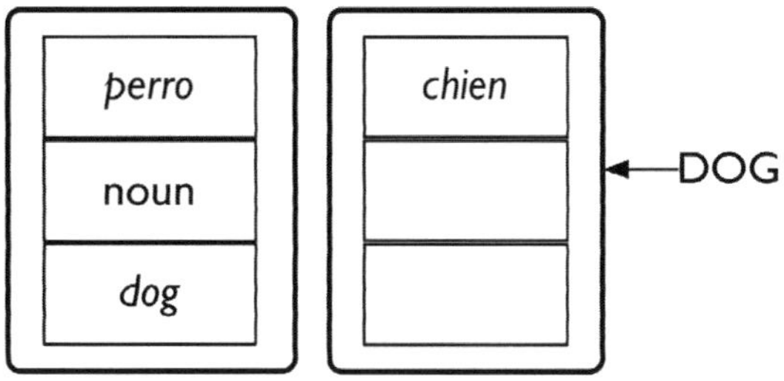

Figure 1: Lexicon sign versus wordlist sign

5.2 Mapping between Form and Concept

A challenge in comparing lexical data among numerous languages is that a complete match between a word's meaning and a general concept rarely occurs within a single language, let alone across languages (Haspelmath and Tadmor, 2009). Therefore, in order to describe the relationship between form and meaning in a wordlist, we use the term *counterpart*, in the sense developed by Haspelmath and Tadmor (2009). This is in contrast to related notions like *definition* or *translation*. While the meanings found in wordlists could, in some cases, be interpreted as definitions or translations, this is not how they are conceived of in their core function. Rather, they are intended to refer to language-independent concepts which have been determined to be a useful way to begin to explore the lexicon of a language.

A key property of the counterpart relationship is that that even if one particular language (e.g., English or Spanish) is used to refer to a particular concept (e.g., MAN), it is not the idiosyncratic semantics of the word in that language that is used to determine the relevant wordlist entry in the target language. For instance, the meaning of the English word MAN is ambiguous between *human* and *male human* but the term in (1) only refers to *human*. In using a language of wider communication, the goal is to find the closest counterpart in the target language for a general concept, not to translate.

We therefore distinguish between the meanings associated with words in a given language from the more general meanings found in wordlists by using the term *concept* for the latter. Thus, a wordlist entry can be schematized as in (2) where a concept and a lexical item are related by the `hasCounterpart` relation. In attested wordlist entries, the concept is, as discussed, most typically indexed via a language of wider communication and a lexical item is indexed via a transcription representing the lexical item's form.

(2) CONCEPT `hasCounterpart` *lexicalItem*

The counterpart relation is, by design, a relatively imprecise one since a lack of precision facilitates the relatively rapid data collection that is considered an important feature of wordlist creation. The meaning of a given counterpart could be broader or narrower than that of the relevant concept, for example (Haspelmath and Tadmor, 2009, p. 9). In principle, the counterpart relation could be made more precise by specifying, for example, that the relevant relation is *sub-counterpart* for cases where a word in a target language refers to a concept narrower than the one referred to in the word list, as illustrated in (3) for English as the target language. There are other logical kinds of counterpart relationships as well (e.g., *super-counterpart*), and the example is primarily for illustrative purposes. In our database, we only employ the counterpart relation since that was the level of precision found in the original data.

(3) PARENT'S SIBLING `hasSubCounterpart` *aunt, uncle*

Though the canonical case for the counterpart relation is that there will be one counterpart for a given concept, this is often not the case in languages and in our data. To take an example from a familiar language, the English counterpart for MOVIE could reasonably be *film* or *movie*, and it is quite easy to imagine a wordlist for English containing both words. The entry in (4) from the dataset we are working with gives an example of this from a wordlist of North Asmat, a language spoken in Indonesia. The concept GRANDFATHER has two counterparts, whose relationship to each other has not been specified in our source.

(4) GRANDFATHER `hasCounterpart` *-ak, afak*

Data like that in (4) has led us to add an additional layer in our model for the mapping between concept and form allowing for the possibility that the mapping may actually refer to a group of forms. With more information, of course, one may be able to avoid mapping to a group of forms by, for example, determining that each member of the group is a sub-counterpart of the relevant concept. However, this information is not available to us in our dataset.

5.3 The Concepticon

The concepts found in wordlists have generally been grouped into informally standardized lists. Within our model, we treat these lists as an object to be modeled in their own right and refer to them as *concepticons* (i.e., "concept lexicon"). As will be discussed in section 6, a concepticon is similar to an interlingua, though this connection has rarely, if ever, been explicitly made.

As understood here, concepticons are simply curated sets of concepts, minimally indexed via one or more words from a language of wider communication but, perhaps, also more elaborately described using multiple languages (e.g., English and Spanish) and illustrative example sentences. Concepticons may include terms for concepts of such general provenance that counterpart words would be expected to occur in almost all languages, such as TO EAT, as well as terms that may occur commonly in only a certain region or language family. For instance, Amazonian languages do not have words for SNOWSHOE or MOSQUE, and Siberian languages do not have a term for TOUCAN (Haspelmath and Tadmor, 2009, p. 5–6).

The concepticon we are employing has been based on three different concept lists. Of these, the most precise and recently published list is the Loanword Typology (LWT) concepticon (Haspelmath and Tadmor, 2009), which consists of 1,460 entries and was developed from the Intercontinental Dictionary Series[2] (IDS) concepticon (1,200 entries). The LWT concepticon often offers more precision for the same concept than the IDS list. For instance, the same concept in both LWT and IDS is described in the LWT list by labeling an English noun with the article *the* (5) in order to clearly distinguish it from a homophonous verb.

(5) **LWT**: THE DUST
IDS: DUST

In addition, certain concepts in the IDS concepticon have been expanded in the LWT list to make it clearer what kinds of words might be treatable as counterparts.

(6) **IDS**: THE LOUSE
LWT: THE LOUSE, HEAD LOUSE, BODY LOUSE

The concepts in LWT and IDS concepticons refer to a wide range of topics but, for historical reasons, they are biased towards the geographical and cultural settings of Europe, southwest Asia, and (native) South America (Haspelmath and Tadmor, 2009, p. 6). The unpublished Usher-Whitehouse concepticon (2,656 entries), used to collect the bulk of the data used in the work described here, includes LWT and IDS concepticons but also adds new concepts, such as WILDEBEEST or WATTLE, in order to facilitate the collection of terms in languages from regions like Africa and Papua New Guinea. Furthermore, certain concepts in the LWT and IDS lists are subdivided in the Usher-Whitehouse concepticon, as shown in (7).

[2]http://lingweb.eva.mpg.de/ids/

(7)
1. **LWT**: TO BREAK
2. **IDS**: BREAK, TR
3. **Usher-Whitehouse**:
   (a) BREAK, INTO PIECES
   (b) BREAK, BY IMPACT
   (c) BREAK, BY MANIPULATION
   (d) BREAK, STRINGS ETC.
   (e) BREAK, LONG OBJECTS
   (f) BREAK, BRITTLE SURFACES

Our unified concepticon combines information from the LWT, IDS, and Usher-Whitehouse lists. This allow us to leverage the advantages of the different lists (e.g., the expanded term list in Usher-Whitehouse against the more detailed concept descriptions of LWT). No wordlist in our database has entries corresponding to all of the concepts in our concepticon. Nonetheless, we now have a dataset with several thousand wordlists whose entries, where present, are linked to the same concepticon, thereby facilitating certain multilingual and cross-lingual applications.

5.4 The Overall Structure of a Wordlist

We schematize our abstract wordlist model in Figure 2. The oval on the left represents the language being described, from which the word forms are drawn (see section 5.1). On the right, the box represents a concepticon (see section 5.3) where the concepts are listed as a set of identifiers (e.g., 1.PERSON) that are associated with labels and related to their best English counterpart. Of course, the labels could be drawn from languages other than English, and other indexing devices, such as pictures, could also be used.

Counterparts from the language being described for the relevant concepts are mapped to blocks of defective signs (most typically containing just one sign, but not always—see section 5.2) which are, in turn, associated with a concept. The schematization further illustrates a possibility not yet explicitly discussed that, due to the relatively imprecise nature of the counterpart relation, one group of forms may be the counterpart for multiple concepts. In short, the mapping between forms and concepts is not necessarily particularly simple.

6 Implementing the Model

We have used the conceptual model for wordlists developed in section 5 to create a wordlist

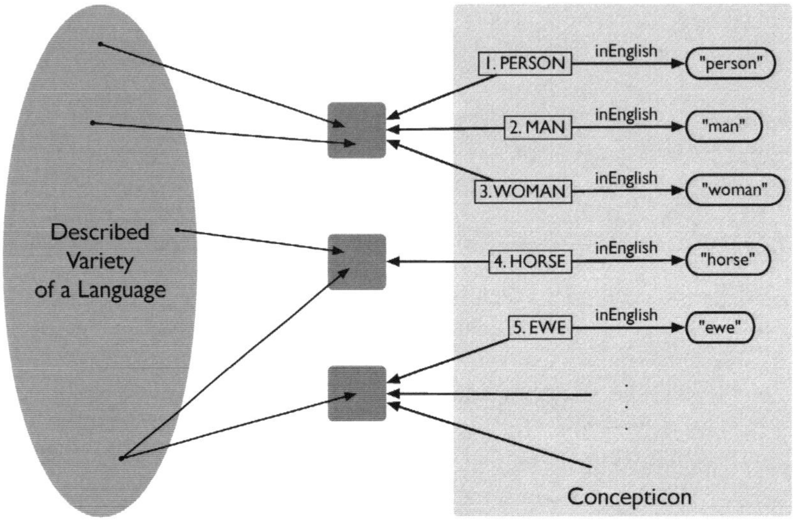

Figure 2: Wordlist modeled as a mapping between a language and a concepticon via blocks of signs

database using Semantic Web technologies, in particular RDF/XML, which we expect to have both research and practical applications.

Each wordlist in our database consists of two components: a set of metadata and a set of entries. The metadata gives the various identifying names and codes for the wordlist e.g., a unique identifier, the ISO 639-3 code, the related Ethnologue language name[3], alternate language names, reference(s), the compilers of the wordlist, etc. All forms in the wordlist are expressed as a sequence of Unicode characters and annotated with appropriate contextual information. In cases where there is more than one form attached to a concept, we create multiple concept-form mappings. We do not explicitly model form groups (see section 2) in our RDF at present since the data we are working with is not sufficiently detailed for us to need to attach information to any particular form group.

Expressing the data encoded in our wordlist database as RDF triples ensures Semantic Web compatibility and allows our work to build on more general work that facilitates sharing and interoperating on linguistic data in a Semantic Web context (Farrar and Lewis, 2007). An RDF fragment describing the wordlist entry in (6) is given in Figure 3 for illustrative purposes. In addition to drawing on standard RDF constructs, we also make use of descriptive linguistic concepts from GOLD[4] (General Ontology for Linguistic Description), which is intended be a sharable OWL ontology for language documentation and description (Farrar and Lewis, 2007). The key data encoded by our RDF representation is the counterpart mapping between a particular wordlist concept (`lego:concept`) drawn from our concepticon and a form (`gold:formUnit`) found in a given wordlist. (The "lego" prefix refers to our internal project namespace.)

An important feature of our RDF encoding is that the counterpart relation does not relate a concept directly to a form but rather to a linguistic sign (`gold:LinguisticSign`) whose form feature contains the relevant specification. This would allow for additional information about the lexical element specified by the given form (e.g., part of speech, definition) to be added to the representation without modification of the model.

Our RDF encoding, at present, is inspired by the traditional understanding of wordlists, building directly on work done by linguists (Haspelmath and Tadmor, 2009). While our use of RDF and an OWL ontology brings the data into a format allowing for much greater interoperability than would otherwise be possible, in order to achieve maximal integration with current efforts in NLP more could be done. For example, we could devise an RDF expression of our model compatible with LMF (Francopoulo et al., 2009) (see section 3).

The most difficult aspect of our model to encode in LMF would appear to be the counterpart relation since core LMF assumes that meanings will be expressed primarily as language-specific *senses*. However, there is work in LMF encod-

[3]`http://ethnologue.com/`

[4]`http://linguistics-ontology.org/`

```
<rdf:RDF xmlns:rdf="http://www.w3.org/1999/02/22-rdf-syntax-ns#"
   xmlns:lego="http://purl.org/linguistics/lego/"
   xmlns:gold="http://purl.org/linguistics/gold/">
  <lego:concept rdf:about= "http://www.purl.org/linguistics/lego/concept/106">
     <lego:hasConceptID>106</lego:hasConceptID>
     <lego:hasConceptLabel>the grandfather</lego:hasConceptLabel>
     <lego:hasSource>LEGO Project Unified Conceptiсon</lego:hasSource>

     <lego:hasCounterpart>
        <gold:LinguisticSign rdf:about=
         "http://www.purl.org/linguistics/North_Asmat_Voorhoeve/12">
          <gold:inLanguage>
           <gold:Language rdf:about=
           "http://www.sil.org/ISO639-3/documentation.asp?id=nks"/>
          </gold:inLanguage>
          <gold:hasForm>
           <gold:formUnit>
             <gold:stringRep>-ak</gold:stringRep>
           </gold:formUnit>
          </gold:hasForm>
          <lego:hasSource>Voorhoeve 1980</lego:hasSource>
        </gold:LinguisticSign>
     </lego:hasCounterpart>

     <lego:hasCounterpart>
        <gold:LinguisticSign rdf:about=
         "http://www.purl.org/linguistics/North_Asmat_Voorhoeve/13">
          <gold:inLanguage>
           <gold:Language rdf:about=
           "http://www.sil.org/ISO639-3/documentation.asp?id=nks"/>
          </gold:inLanguage>
          <gold:hasForm>
           <gold:formUnit>
             <gold:stringRep>afak</gold:stringRep>
           </gold:formUnit>
          </gold:hasForm>
          <lego:hasSource>Voorhoeve 1980</lego:hasSource>
        </gold:LinguisticSign>
     </lego:hasCounterpart>
  </lego:concept>
</rdf:RDF>
```

Figure 3: Wordlist Entry RDF Fragment

ing something quite comparable to our notion of counterpart, namely a *SenseAxis*, intended to support interlingual pivots for multilingual resources (Soria et al., 2009).

As discussed in section 3, the concept labels used in traditional wordlists can be understood as a kind of interlingua. Therefore, it seems that a promising approach for adapting our model to an LMF model would involve making use of the SenseAxes. Because of this we believe that it would be relatively straightforward to adapt our database in a way which would make it even more accessible for NLP applications than it is in its present form, though we leave this as a task for future work.

7 Evaluation

We have identified the following dimensions across which it seems relevant to evaluate our work against the state of the art: (i) the extent to which it can be applied generally to wordlist data, (ii) how it compares to existing wordlist databases, (iii) how it compares to other work which develops data models intended to serve as targets for migration of legacy linguistic data, and (iv) the extent to which our model can create lexical data that can straightforwardly interoperate with other lexical data. We discuss each of these dimensions of evaluation in turn.

(i) The RDF/XML model described here has been successfully used to represent the entire core dataset being used for this project (see section 2). This represents around 2,700 wordlists and half a million forms, suggesting the model is reasonable, at least as a first attempt. Further testing will require attempting to incorporate wordlist data from other sources into our model.

(ii) Wordlists databases have been constructed for comparative linguistic work for decades. However, there have not been extensive systematic attempts to encode them in interoperable formats to the best of our knowledge, and certainly not involving a dataset of the size explored here. The only comparable project is found in the World Loanword Database (Haspelmath and Tadmor, 2010) (WOLD) which includes, as a possibility, an RDF/XML export. This feature of the database is not explicitly documented, making a direct comparison difficult. An examination of the data produced makes it appear largely similar to the model proposed here. The database itself covers many fewer languages (around 40) but has much more data for each of its entries. In any event, we believe our project and WOLD are roughly similar regarding the extent to which the produced resources can be used for multiple purposes, though it is difficult to examine this in detail at this time in the absence of better documentation of WOLD.

(iii) As discussed in section 3, most work on designing data models to facilitate migration of legacy descriptive data to more modern formats has used representative data rather than producing a substantial new resource in its own right. Furthermore, while the data models have been general in nature, the data encoding has often been in parochial XML formats. By producing a substantial resource in a Semantic Web encoding in parallel with the data modeling, we believe our results exceed most of the comparable work on legacy linguistic data, with the exception of ODIN (Xia and Lewis, 2009) which has also produced a substantial resource.

(iv) Finally, by building our wordlist model around the abstract notion of the linguistic sign, and explicitly referring to the concept of sign through an OWL ontology, we believe we have produced a wordlist data model which can produce data which can straightforwardly interoperate with data from full lexicons since lexicon entries, too, can be modeled as signs, as in Figure 1.

Therefore, while our work cannot be straightforwardly evaluated with quantitative metrics, we believe that on a qualitative level it can be evaluated at or above the state of the art across several key dimensions.

8 Applications

Unlike typical research in NLP, our dataset covers thousands of minority languages that are otherwise poorly represented. Therefore, while our data is sparse in many ways, it has a coverage well-beyond what is normally found.

Crucially, our data model makes visible the similarities between a conceptícon and an interlingua, thus opening up a data type produced for descriptive linguistics for use in NLP contexts. In particular, we have created a resource that we believe could be exploited for NLP applications where simple word-to-word mapping across languages is useful, as in the PanImages[5] search of the PanLex project, which facilitates cross-lingual image searching. Such a database can also be readily exploited for machine identification of cognates and recurrent sound correspondences to test algorithms for language family reconstruction (Kondrak et al., 2007; Nerbonne et al., 2007) or to assist in the automatic identification of phonemic systems and, thereby, enhance relevant existing work (Moran and Wright, 2009). We, therefore, think it represents a useful example of using data modeling and legacy data conversion to find common ground between descriptive linguistics and NLP.

Acknowledgments

Funding for the work described here was provided by NSF grant BCS-0753321, and the work is being done in the context of the larger Lexicon Enhancement via the GOLD Ontology project, headed by researchers at the Institute for Language Information and Technology at Eastern Michigan University. Partial funding for the collection and curation of the wordlists was provided by the Rosetta Project (NSF DUE-0333727), along with the Max Planck Institute for Evolutionary Anthropology.

References

Alison Alvarez, Lori Levin, Robert Frederking, Simon Fung, Donna Gates, and Jeff Good. 2006. The MILE corpus for less commonly taught languages. In *NAACL '06: Proceedings of the Human Language Technology Conference of the NAACL, Companion Volume*, pages 5–8. ACL.

[5] `http://www.panimages.org/`

John Bell and Steven Bird. 2000. A preliminary study of the structure of lexicon entries. In *Proceedings from the Workshop on Web-Based Language Documentation and Description*. Philadelphia, December 12–15, 2000.

Emily M. Bender, Dan Flickinger, and Stephan Oepen. 2002. The Grammar Matrix: An open-source starter-kit for the rapid development of cross-linguistically consistent broad-coverage precision grammars. In John Carroll, Nelleke Oostdijk, and Richard Sutcliffe, editors, *Proceedings of the Workshop on Grammar Engineering and Evaluation at the 19th International Conference on Computational Linguistics*, pages 8–14, Taipei, Taiwan.

Steven Bird and Gary Simons. 2003. Seven dimensions of portability for language documention and description. *Language*, 79:557–582.

Scott Farrar and William D. Lewis. 2007. The GOLD Community of Practice: An infrastructure for linguistic data on the Web. *Language Resources and Evaluation*, 41:45–60.

Gil Francopoulo, Nuria Bel, Monte George, Nicoletta Calzolari, Monica Monachini, Mandy Pet, and Claudia Soria. 2009. Multilingual resources for NLP in the lexical markup framework (LMF). *Language Resources and Evaluation*, 43:57–70.

Jeff Good. 2004. The descriptive grammar as a (meta)database. In *Proceedings of the E-MELD Workshop on Linguistic Databases and Best Practice*. Detroit, Michigan.

Martin Haspelmath and Uri Tadmor. 2009. The Loanword Typology Project and the World Loanword Database. *Loanwords in the world's languages: A comparative handbook*, pages 1–33. Berlin: De Gruyter.

Martina Haspelmath and Uri Tadmor, editors. 2010. *World Loanword Database*. Munich: Max Planck Digital Library. http://wold.livingsources.org.

Nancy Ide, Daniel Greenstein, and Piek Vossen. 1998. Introduction to EuroWordNet. *Computers and the Humanities*, 32:73–89.

Grzegorz Kondrak, David Beck, and Philip Dilts. 2007. Creating a comparative dictionary of Totonac-Tepehua. In *Proceedings of Ninth Meeting of the ACL Special Interest Group in Computational Morphology and Phonology*, pages 134–141. ACL.

Steven Moran and Richard Wright. 2009. *Phonetics Information Base and Lexicon (PHOIBLE)*. http://phoible.org.

John Nerbonne, T. Mark Ellison, and Grzegorz Kondrak. 2007. Computing and historical phonology. In *Proceedings of Ninth Meeting of the ACL Special Interest Group in Computational Morphology and Phonology*, pages 1–5. ACL.

Sergei Nirenburg, Marge McShane, and Steve Beale. 2004. The rationale for building resources expressly for NLP. In *4th International Conference on Language Resources and Evaluation*, Lisbon, Portugal.

Sebastian Nordhoff. 2008. Electronic reference grammars for typology: Challenges and solutions. *Language Documentation & Conservation*, 2:296–324.

Tom O'Hara, Kavi Mahesh, and Sergei Nirenburg. 1998. Lexical Acquisition with WordNet and the Mikrokosmos Ontology. *In Proceedings of the ACL Workshop on the Use of WordNet in NLP*, pages 94–101.

Alexis Palmer and Katrin Erk. 2007. IGT-XML: An XML format for interlinearized glossed text. In *Proceedings of the Linguistic Annotation Workshop*, pages 176–183. ACL.

Alexis Palmer, Taesun Moon, and Jason Baldridge. 2009. Evaluating automation strategies in language documentation. In *Proceedings of the NAACL HLT 2009 Workshop on Active Learning for Natural Language Processing*, pages 36–44. ACL.

Francesco Ronzano, Maurizio Tesconi, Salvatore Minutoli, Andrea Marchetti. 2010. Collaborative management of KYOTO Multilingual Knowledge Base: The Wikyoto Knowledge Editor. In *Proceedings of the 5th International Conference of the Global WordNet Association (GWC-2010)*. Mumbai, India.

Gary Simons, Brian Fitzsimons, Terence Langendoen, William Lewis, Scott Farrar, Alexis Lanham, Ruby Basham, and Hector Gonzalez. 2004. The descriptive grammar as a (meta)database. In *Proceedings of the E-MELD Workshop on Linguistic Databases and Best Practice*. Detroit, Michigan.

Claudia Soria, Monica Monachini, and Piek Vossen. 2009. Wordnet-LMF: Fleshing out a Standardized Format for Wordnet Interoperability. In *International Workshop on Intercultural Collaboration (IWIC)*, pages 139–146. ACM.

Tokunaga Takenobu, Nicoletta Calzolari, Chu-Ren Huang, Laurent Prevot, Virach Sornlertlamvanich, Monica Monachini, Xia YingJu, Shirai Kiyoaki, Thatsanee Charoenporn, Claudia Soria, and Hao, Yu. 2006. Infrastructure for standardization of Asian language resources In *Proceedings of the COLING/ACL Main Conference Poster Sessions*, pages 827–834. ACL.

Piek Vossen. 2004. EuroWordNet: A multilingual database of autonomous and language-specific wordnets connected via an Inter-Lingual-Index. *International Journal of Lexicography*, 17:161–173.

Fei Xia and William D. Lewis. 2009. Applying NLP technologies to the collection and enrichment of language data on the Web to aid linguistic research. In *LaTeCH-SHELT&R '09: Proceedings of the EACL 2009 Workshop on Language Technology and Resources for Cultural Heritage, Social Sciences, Humanities, and Education*, pages 51–59. ACL.

Evidentiality for Text Trustworthiness Detection

Qi Su[1, 2], Chu-Ren Huang and Helen Kai-yun Chen
[1]Depart of Chinese & Bilingual Studies, The Hong Kong Polytechnic University
[2]Key Laboratory of Computational Linguistics, Peking University
sukia@pku.edu.cn, {helenkychen, churen.huang}@gmail.com

Abstract

Evidentiality is the linguistic representation of the nature of evidence for a statement. In other words, it is the linguistically encoded evidence for the trustworthiness of a statement. In this paper, we aim to explore how linguistically encoded information of evidentiality can contribute to the prediction of trustworthiness in natural language processing (NLP). We propose to incorporate evidentiality into a framework of machine learning based text classification. We first construct a taxonomy of evidentials. Then experiments involving collaborative question answering (CQA) are designed and implemented using this taxonomy. The experimental results confirm that evidentiality is an important clue for text trustworthiness detection. With the binarized vector setting, evidential based text representation model has considerably performaned better than both the bag-of-word model and the content word based model. Most crucially, we show that the best trustworthiness detection result is achieved when evidentiality is incorporated in a linguistically sophisticated model where their meanings are interpreted in both semantic and pragmatic terms.

1 Introduction

With the exponential increase in web sites and documents, the amount of information is no longer a main concern for automatic knowledge acquisition. This trend raises, however, at least two new issues. The first is how to locate the information which exactly meets our needs among the vast web content. Efforts to address this issue can be exemplified by advanced research in information retrieval, information extraction, etc. The second is how to judge the validity of the acquired information, that is, the trustworthiness of information. This issue has attracted considerable interest in some related research areas recently. Taking the specific information retrieval task, question answering (QA) as an example, a QA system attempts to retrieve the most appropriate answers to questions from web resources. To determine the trustworthiness of the extracted candidate answers, a common approach is to exploit the co-occurrence frequency of questions and candidate answers. That is, if a candidate answer co-occurs more frequently with the question than other candidates, the QA system may judge it as the best answer (Magnini, 2002). This approach presupposes and relies crucially on information redundancy. Although this heuristic method is simple and straightforward, it is not applicable to all cases. For the applications which don't involve much information redundancy, the heuristic could cease to be effective. The task of collaborative question answering (CQA) which we will address in this paper is just one of such examples. For a user posted question, there are usually only few answers provided. So, the heuristic is not useful in providing the best answer. In addition, since the spread of unsubstantiated rumors on the Internet is so pervasive, the high-frequency information on the Web sometimes may mislead the judgment of trustworthiness. In terms of the above consideration, it is essential to look for other approaches which allow directly modeling of the trustworthiness of a text.

Given that non-textual features (such as user's Web behavior) used in text trustworthiness detection are often manipulated by information providers, as well as no directly related textual features for the task has been proposed up to

Proceedings of the 2010 Workshop on NLP and Linguistics: Finding the Common Ground, ACL 2010, pages 10–17,
Uppsala, Sweden, 16 July 2010.

date, we need a more felicitous model for detecting the trustworthiness of statements. Noting that *evidentiality* is often linguistically encoded and hence provides inherent information on trustworthiness for a statement, we propose to incorporate the linguistic model of evidentiality in our study. Specifically, we incorporate evidentiality into a machine learning based text classification framework, and attempt to verify the validity of evidentiality in trustworthiness prediction of text information in the context of collaborative question answering. The experimental results show that evidentials are important clues in predicting the trustworthiness of text. Since none of the task-specific heuristics has been incorporated, the current approach could also be easily adapted to fit other natural language processing applications.

The paper proceeds as follows. In section 2 we discuss related work on text trustworthiness detection. The section is divided into two parts: the current methodology and the textual features for analysis in the task. Section 3 introduces the linguistic researches on evidentiality and our taxonomy of evidentials based on the trustworthiness indication. Section 4 presents the experiment settings and results. Finally, in section 5 we discuss the experiment results and conclude the current research.

2 Related Work

The research of text trustworthiness is very helpful for many other natural language processing applications. For example, in their research on question answering, Banerjee and Han (2009) modulate answer grade by using a weighted combination of the original score and answer credibility evaluation. Also, Weerkamp and Rijke (2008) incorporate textual credibility indicators in the retrieval process to improve topical blog posts retrieval. Gyongyi et al (2004) propose a TrustRank algorithm for semi-automatically separating reputable, good Web pages from spams.

2.1 General Approaches for Text Trustworthiness Detection

In past research, the judgment for the trustworthiness or credibility of a given text content is usually tackled from two aspects: entity oriented and content oriented (Rubin and Liddy, 2005). The former approach takes into consideration the information providers' individual profiles, such as their identity, reputation, authority and past web behavior; whereas the latter approach considers the actual content of texts. Metzger (2007) reviews several cognitive models of credibility assessment and points out that credibility is a multifaceted concept with two primary dimensions: expertise and trustworthiness. Following Matzger's framework, Rubin and Liddy (2005) compile a list of factors that users may take into account in assessing credibility of blog sites. This list could also be summarized as the above mentioned two-folds: the bloggers' profiles and the information posted in the entries.

Comparing these two aspects, most existing research on text trustworthiness focuses on the user oriented features. Lots of user oriented features have been proposed in the research of credibility detection. To score the user oriented features such as user's authority, a common approach is based on a graph-based ranking algorithm such as HITS and PageRank (Zhang et al, 2007; Bouguessa et al, 2008).

In the research of text trustworthiness detection, the overwhelmingly adaption of non-textual features such as entity profiles over text content based features reflect some researchers' belief that superficial textual features cannot meet the need of text credibility identification (Jeon et al, 2006). In this paper, we examine the lexical semantic feature of evidential and argue that evidentiality, as a linguistically instantiated representation of quality of information content, offers a robust processing model for text trustworthiness detection.

The detection of information trustworthiness also has promising application values. Google News [1] is just such an application that ranks search results according to the credibility of the news. Other online news aggregation service, such as NewTrust [2], also focuses on providing users with credible and high quality news and stories. The existed applications, however, rely on either the quality of web sites or user voting. So, it is anticipated that the improvement on the technology of text trustworthiness detection by incorporating lexical semantic cues such as evidentiality may shed light on these applications.

2.2 Textual Feature Based Text Trustworthiness Detection

Although non-textual features have been popular in text credibility detection, there has been a few research focusing on textual features so far. Gil

[1] http://news.google.com/

[2] http://www.newstrust.net/

and Artz (2006) argue that the degree of trust in an entity is only one ingredient in deciding whether or not to trust the information it provides. They further point out that entity-centered issues are made with respect to publicly available data and services, and thus will not be possible in many cases. In their research of topical blog posts retrieval, Weerkamp and Rijke (2008) also consider only textual credibility indicators since they mentioned that additional resources (such as bloggers' profiles) is hard to obtain for technical or legal reasons.

However, most research which utilizes textual features in text trustworthiness detection usually equates writing quality of document with its trustworthiness. Therefore, some secondary features which may not directly related to trustworthiness are proposed, including spelling errors, the lack of leading capitals, the large number of exclamation markers, personal pronouns and text length (Weerkamp and Rijke, 2008). There has not been attempted to directly evaluate inherent linguistic cues for trustworthiness of a statement.

3 On Evidentiality in Text

Evidentiality, as an explicit linguistic system to encode quality of information, offers obvious and straightforward evidence for text trustworthiness detection. Yet it has not attracted the attention which it deserves in most of the natural language processing studies. In this paper, we aim to explore how we can incorporate the linguistic model of evidentiality into a robust and efficient machine learning based text classification framework.

Aikhenvald (2003) observes that every language has some way of making reference to the source of information. Once the language is being used, it always imprinted with the subjective relationship from the speakers towards the information. Evidentiality is information providers' specifications for the information sources and their attitudes toward the information. As a common linguistic phenomenon to all the languages, it has attracted linguists' attention since the beginning of 20th century. In any language, evidentiality is a semantic category which could be expressed on both grammatical level (as in some American Indian language) and lexical level (as in English, Chinese and many other languages). The linguistic expressions of evidentiality are named as evidentials or evidential markers.

Mushin (2000) defines evidential as a marker which qualifies the reliability of information. It is an explicit expression of the speaker's attitudes toward the trustworthiness of information source. For instance,

a). *It's probably raining.*
b). *It must be raining.*
c). *It sounds like it's raining.*
d). *I think/guess/suppose it's raining.*
e). *I can hear/see/feel/smell it raining.*

It is obvious that the information provided in the above examples is subjective. The information expresses the personal experience or attitudes, while at the same time reflects the speakers' estimation for the trustworthiness of the statement by information providers.

3.1 The Definition of Evidentiality

There are two dimensions of the linguistic definition for evidentiality. The term evidentiality is originally introduced by Jakobson (1957) as a label for the verbal category indicating the alleged source of information about the narrated events. In line with Jakobson's definition, the narrow definition of evidentiality proposed by other researchers focuses mainly on the specification of the information sources, that is, the evidence through which information is acquired (DeLancey, 2001). Comparing with the narrow definition, the board definition explains evidentiality in a much wider sense, and characterizes evidentiality as expressions of speaker's attitude toward information, typically expressed by modalities (Chafe, 1986; Mushin, 2000).

Ifantidou (2001) also holds that evidential has two main functions: 1) indicating the source of knowledge; 2) indicating the speaker's degree of certainty about the proposition expressed. He further divides them in details as follows.

a) Information can be acquired in various ways, including observation (e.g. *see*), hearsay (e.g. *hear, reportedly*), inference (e.g. *must, deduce*), memory (e.g. *recall*).

b) Evidentiality can indicate the speaker's degree of certainty, including certain propositional attitude (e.g. *think, guess*) and adverbials (e.g. *certainly, surely*), also epistemic models (e.g. *may, ought to*).

3.2 The Taxonomy of Evidentials

Evidentiality has its hierarchy which forms a continuum that marks from the highest to the least trustworthiness. Up to now, there are many hierarchical schemes proposed by researchers.

	Absolute	High	Moderate	Low
Attributive/modal adverb	*certainly, sure, of course, definitely, absolutely, undoubtedly*	*clearly, obviously, apparently, really, always*	*Seemingly, probably*	*maybe, personally, perhaps, possibly, presumably*
Lexical verb	*report, certain*	*believe, see*	*seem, think, sound*	*doubt, wish, wonder, infer, assume, forecast, fell, heard*
Auxiliary verb		*must*	*ought, should, would, could, can*	*may, might*
Epistemic adjective	*definite*		*possible, likely, unlikely, probable, positive, potential*	*not sure, doubtful*

Table 1. The Categorization and Inside Items of Evidentiality

Oswalt (1986) suggests a priority hierarchy of evidentials as:

Performative > *Factual* > *Visual* > *Auditory* > *Inferential* > *Quotative*

In this evidential hierarchy, *performative* carries the highest degree of trustworthiness since Oswalt considers that the speaker is speaking of the act he himself is performing. It is the most reliable source of evidence for the knowledge of that event.

Whereas Barners (1984) proposes the following hierarchy:

Visual > *Non-visual* > *Apparent* > *Second-hand* > *Assumed*

He points out that visual evidence takes precedence over the auditory evidence and is more reliable.

The above two hierarchies are based on the narrow definition of evidentiality mentioned above. There are also some hierarchies involving the board definition of evidentiality, such as Chafe (1986)'s categories of evidentiality.

In this paper, we adopt a broad definition of evidentiality and focus on a trustworthiness categorization. This categorization follows the model of four-dimensional certainty categorization by Rubin et al (2005). In this model, it is suggested that the division of the certainty level dimension into four categories - *Absolute*, *High*, *Moderate* and *Low*. With some revision, there are different items of evidential words and phrased that we extracted from the corpus. These items from each category to be adopted in our experiments are presented in Table 1.

4 Incorporating Evidentiality into Machine Learning for Trustworthiness Detection

In this section, we apply evidentiality in an actual implement of text trustworthiness detection. It is based on a specific web application service, collaborative question answering (CQA), in which the trustworthiness of text content is very helpful for finding the best answers in the service.

With the development of Web2.0, the services of CQA in community media have largely attracted people's attention. Comparing with the general ad hoc information searching, question answering could help in finding the most accurate answers extracted from the vast web content. Whereas in the collaborative question answering, the CQA community media just provide a web space in which users can freely post their questions, and at the same time other users may answer these questions based on their knowledge and interests. Due to the advantage of interactivity, CQA usually could settle some questions which cannot be dealt with by ad hoc information retrieval. However, since the platform is open to anyone, the quality of the answers provided by users is hard to identify. People may present answers of various qualities due to the limitation of their knowledge, attitude and purpose of answering the questions. As a result, the issue of how to identify the most trustworthy answers from the user-provided content turns out to be the most challenging part to the system.

As mentioned previously, the trustworthiness of text content could be identified from two dimensions. The first one relies on the features related with information distributors. The second one relies on the content of a text. In current research we focus on textual features, especially the feature of evidentiality in texts. The feature will be incorporated into a machine learning based text classification framework in order to identify the best answers for CQA questions.

4.1 The Dataset

For the experiments, we use the snapshot of Yahoo! Answers dataset which is crawled by Emory University[3]. Since our experiments only involve text features, we use the answer parts from it without considering the question sets and user profiles. Such information could be incorporated to achieve a higher performance in the future.

With regard to the text classification problems, there is typically a substantial class distribution skew (Forman, 2003). For the Yahoo! Answers dataset, a question only has one best answer and accordingly all the other answers will be marked as non-best answers. Thus the class of best answer contains much fewer texts than the class of non-best answers. In our dataset (a proportion of the overall CQA dataset provided by Emory University), the number of best answers is 2,165, and the number of non-best answers is 17,654. The proportion of the size of the two answer sets is around 1:8.15, showing a significant skews. For a better comparison of experimental results, we use a balanced dataset which is generated from a normal distribution dataset.

A 10-fold validation is used for the evaluation, where the datasets of best and non-best answers are divided into 10 subsets of approximately equal size respectively. In the normally distributed dataset, we use one of the ten subsets as the test set, while the other nine are combined together to from the training set. In the balanced dataset, for each subset of the non-best answers, we only use the first *k* answers, in which *k* is the size of each subset of best answers. The training data and test data used in the machine learning process are shown in Table 2.

	Training /Test Set	Best answer	Non-best answer
normal distribution dataset	training	19,490	158,889
	test	2,165	17,654
balanced dataset	training	19,490	19,490
	test	2,165	2,165

Table 2. The Dataset Used for the Experiments

4.2 Experiment Settings

To conduct a machine learning based classification for best answers and non-best answers, we first need to construct the feature vectors. The representation of text is the core issue in the machine learning model for text classification. In text domains, feature selection plays an essential role to make the learning task efficient and more accurate. As the baseline comparison, we use the following feature vector settings.

• **Baseline1** represents using all the words in the text as features (when the frequency of the word in the dataset is bigger than a predefined threshold *j*).

• **Baseline2** represents using all the content words (here we include the four main categories of content words - nouns, verbs, adjectives and adverbs identified by a POS tagger) in the dataset as features.

We use both the above two baselines. The bag-of-word model of Baseline1 is a conventional method in text representation. However, since not all the words are linguistically significant, in Baseline2, we consider only the content words in the dataset, since content words convey the core meaning of a sentence.

For the evidentiality-based classification, we adopt the following feature vector settings.

• **Evidential** represents using all the evidentials in text as features.

• **Evidential'** represents using all the evidentials except for those in the category of *Moderate* as features.

• **Evid.cat4** represents using the four evidentiality categories of *Absolute*, *High*, *Moderate* and *Low* from Table 1.

• **Evid.cat2** represents using the two categories of *Absolute* and *High* as the positive evidential and *Moderate* and *Low* as the negative evidential.

• **Evid.cat2'** omits the evidential category of *Moderate*, and represents using the two categories of *Absolute* and *High* as the positive evidential and only the category of *Low* as the negative evidential feature.

Some researchers have proved that usually a Boolean indicator of whether the feature item occurred in the document is sufficient for classification (Forman, 2003). Although there are also some other feature weighting schemes such as term frequency (TF), document frequency (DF), etc, comparison of these different weighting schemes is not the object of the current research. So in this paper, we only consider Boolean weighting. In the Boolean text representation model, each feature represents the Boolean occurrence of a word, evidential, or evidential category according to the different feature settings. By the experimental settings, we want to verify the hypothesis that incorporating the knowledge

[3] http://ir.mathcs.emory.edu/shared

of evidentiality into text representation can lead to improvement in classification performance.

In our experiment, we perform text preprocessing including word segmentation and part-of-speech (POS) tagging. The Stanford Log-linear Part-Of-Speech Tagger (http://nlp.stanford.edu/software/tagger.shtml) is used for POS tagging. We adopt support vector machine (SVM) as the machine learning model to classify best answers from non-best ones, and use the SVMlight package (http://svmlight.joachims.org) as the classifier with the default parameters and a linear kernel. For the evaluation, we use the metrics of precision (**Prec.** as in table 3), recall (**Rec.** as in table 3), accuracy (**Acc.** as in table 3) and **F1**: F_1-measure, the harmonic mean of the precision and recall.

4.3 Evaluation

Table 3 shows the experimental results using the balanced dataset with Boolean weighting. The focus of the experiment evaluation is on identifying the best answers, so the evaluation metrics are all for the best answers collection. From the table, we see increases of the two feature vector setting of evidentials over both baseline results. The highest improvement is 14.85%, achieved by the feature set of Evidential'. However, there is no increase found in the settings of using evidential categories. This means that although the category of evidentials in indicating text trustworthiness is obvious for human, it is not necessary a preferred feature for machine learning.

	Prec.	Rec.	Acc.	F1
Baseline1	45.62%	51.51%	45.15%	47.94%
Baseline2	59.58%	39.20%	56.30%	47.28%
Evidential	67.78%	44.18%	61.59%	**53.49%**
Evidential'	47.40%	90.12%	45.06%	**62.13%**
Evid.cat4	64.15%	25.85%	55.70%	36.85%
Evid.cat2	60.86%	28.21%	55.03%	38.55%
Evid.cat2'	40.35%	25.85%	43.81%	31.51%

Table 3. Experimental Results Using the Balanced Training/Test Dataset (with Boolean Weighting)

To eliminate the potential effect of term weighting scheme on performance trend among different text representation models, we also conduct experiments using TF weighting. By the experiments, we aim to compare the relative performances of different feature vectors constructed with evidentials, and the results are demonstrated in Table 4.

	Prec.	Rec.	Acc.	F1
Evidential	66.78%	45.57%	61.45%	**54.17%**
Evidential'	59.66%	20.82%	53.37%	30.87%
Evid.cat4	50.00%	18.14%	50.00%	26.63%
Evid.cat2	55.91%	16.39%	51.73%	25.35%

Table 4. Experimental Results Using the Balanced Training/Test Dataset (with TF Weighting)

From the table, it can be observed that using evidentials as features shows better improvement in the performance than the category of evidentials as a feature. A similar performance has been summarized in Table 3.

Finally, but not the least, to better understand the effect of evidential category on the machine learning performance, we design additional experiments as follows.

- **Evid_cat1** stands for combining the four evidential categories into one, and uses only this one category of evidential as a feature. The approach of Boolean weighting is actually the same as a rule-based approach that classifies the test dataset according to whether evidential occurs or not.

BOOL	Prec.	Rec.	Acc.	F1
Evid_cat1	59.42%	61.59%	59.76%	60.49%

Table 5. Experimental Results Using the Balanced Training/Test Dataset (with Boolean Weighting; Only One Evidential Category)

Table 5 presents a set of interesting experimental result. In the result, all the four evaluation metrics show performance increases comparing to the baseline, and it even outperforms almost all the other results from both weighting schemes. Based on this result, it is suggested that evidentiality still may contribute to the task of text trustworthiness detection. Moreover, it can significantly reduce the dimensionality of feature space (e.g. for Baseline 1, the dimensionality of feature dimension is 218,328 in one of our cases; while for the experiment of Evidential, it reduced to only 51 as shown in Table

1). However, we should address the question of why not all types of evidential features demonstrate improvement of detection. We will further discuss the issue from a pragmatic viewpoint in the next section.

5 Conclusion and Discussion

In this paper, we propose to incorporate the linguistic knowledge of evidentiality in the NLP task of trustworthiness prediction. As evidentiality is an integral and inherent part of any statement and explicitly expresses information about the trustworthiness of this statement, it should provide the most robust and direct model for trustworthiness detection. We first set up the taxonomy of lexical evidentials. By incorporating evidentiality into a machine learning based text classification framework, we conduct experiments for a specific application, CQA. The evidentials in the dataset are extracted to form different text representation schemes. Our experimental results using evidentials show improvements up to 14.85% over the baselines. However, not all types of evidential features contributed to the improvement of detection. We also compared the effect of different types of evidential based feature representation schemes on the classification performance.

The way to model evidentiality for trustworthiness detection which we adopted in our initial experiment design actually could also be explained by Grice's Maxim of Quality: be truthful. As the Maxim of Quality requires one "not to say that for which one lacks adequate evidence", we hypothesize that evidential constructions mark the adequacy of evidence and should indicate reliable answers. However, the results from our experiments only partially supported this hypothesis. The results showed a satisfactory performance was achieved when all evidential markers were treated as negative evidence for reliability. This result could then be accounted by invoking another Gricean maxim: Quantity.

The Maxim of Quantity requires that "one makes his/her contribution as informative as is required, and at the same time does not make the contribution more informative than is required." As evidentiality is not grammaticalized in English, the use of evidentiality is not a required grammatical element. An answer marked by evidentials would violate Maxim of Quantity if it is correct. The Maxim of Quantity predicts that good answers are plain statements without evidential markers. On the frequent use of evidential markers for less reliable answers can be accounted for by speakers' attempt to follow both Maxims of Quality and Quantity. The evidential marks are used to compensate for the fact that speakers are not very confident about the answer, yet would like to adhere to the Maxim of Quality. In other words, evidentials are not likely to be used in reliable answers because of the Maxim of Quality, but it is likely used in less reliable answers because the speakers may try to provide proof of adequate evidence by a grammatical device instead of providing true answer.

Therefore, this model elaborated above takes into account not only the grammatical function of evidential constructions but also how this linguistic structure is used as a pragmatic/discourse device. In other words, this study suggests that modeling linguistic theory in NLP needs to take a more comprehensive approach than the simple modular approach where only one module (based on evidentiality) is used. Linguistic modeling needs to consider both how linguistic structure/knowledge is represented and processed, we also need to model how a particular linguistic device in use.

In the further works, we plan to continue developing and elaborate on a multi-modular linguistic model of evidentiality for knowledge acquisition. We will also explore the possibility of incorporating other features, both textual and non-textual, to further improve performances in the tasks of text trustworthiness detection.

References

Agichtein E, Castillo C, and etc. 2008. Finding high-quality content in social media. In *Proceedings of WSDM2008*.

Aikhenvald A and Dixon, ed. 2003. *Studies in evidentiality*. Amsterdam/Philadelphia: John Benjamins Publishing Company

Banerjee P, Han H. 2009. Credibility: A Language Modeling Approach to Answer Validation, In *Proceedings of NAACL HLT 2009*, Boulder, Bolorado, US

Barners J. 1984. Evidentials in the Tuyuca Verb. IN *International Journal of American Linguistics*, 50

Bouguessa M, Dumoulin B, Wang S. 2008. Identifying Authoritative Actors in Question-Answering Forums - The Case of Yahoo! Answers, In *Proceedings of KDD'08*, Las Vegas, Nevada, USA

Chafe W. 1986. Evidentiality: The Linguistic Coding of Epistemology, Evidentiality in English Conversation and Academic Writing. In Chafe and Nichols, (ed.). *Evidentiality: The Linguistic Coding of Epistemology*. Norwood, NJ: Ablex

DeLancey S. 2001. The mirative and evidentiality. In *Journal of Pragmatic*, 33

Forman G. 2003. An Extensive Empirical Study of Feature Selection Metrics for Text Classification, In *Journal of Machine Learning Research*, 3

Gil Y, Artz D. 2006. Towards Content Trust of Web Resources, In *Proceedings of the 15th International World Wide Web Conference*, Edinburgh, Scotland

Gyongyi Z, Molina H, Pedersen J. 2004. Combating Web Spam with TrustRank. In *Proceedings of the 30th VLDB Conference*, Toronto, Canada

Ifantidou E. 2001. Evidentials and Relevance. *John Benjamins Publishing Company.*

Jeon J, Croft W, Lee J and Park S. 2006. A Framework to Predict the Quality of Answers with Non-textual Features, In *Proceedings of SIGIR'06*, Seattle, Washington, USA

Leopold E, Kindermann J. 2002. Text Categorization with Support Vector Machines. How to Represent Texts in Input Space?, In *Machine Learning*, 46, 423-444

Oswalt R. 1986. The evidential system of Kashaya. IN Chafe W and Nichols (Eds.), *Evidentiality: The linguistic coding of epistemology*. Norwood, NJ: Ablex

Rubin V, Liddy E, Kando N. 2005. Certainty Identification in Texts: Categorization Model and Manual Tagging Results, In Shanahan J and et al (Eds.), *Computing Attitude and Affect in Text: Theory and Applications* (*The Information Retrieval Series*): Springer-Verlag New York, Inc.

Rubin V, Liddy E. 2006. Assessing Credibility of Weblogs, In *Proceedings of the AAAI Spring Symposium: Computational Approaches to Analyzing Weblogs (CAAW)*

Magnini B, Negri M, Prevete R and Tanev H. 2002. Is It the Right Answer? Exploiting Web Redundancy for Answer Validation, In *Proceedings of the 40th Annual Meeting of the Association for Computational Linguistics*, Philadelphia, PA

Metzger M. 2007. Evaluating Online Information and Recommendations for Future Research, *Journal of the American Society for Information Science and Technology*, 58(13)

Mushin I. 2000. Evidentiality and Deixis in Retelling, In *Journal of Pragmatics*, 32

Weerkamp W, Rijke M. 2008. Credibility Improves Topical Blog Post Retrieval. In *Proceedings of ACL08: HLT*

Zhang J, Ackerman M, Adamic L. 2007. Expertise Networks in Online Communities: Structure and Algorithms. In *Proceedings of the 16th ACM International World Wide Web Conference (WWW'07)*

On the Role of NLP in Linguistics

Dipti Misra Sharma
Language Technologies Research Centre
IIIT-H, Hyderabad, India
dipti@iiit.ac.in

Abstract

This paper summarizes some of the applications of NLP techniques in various linguistic sub-fields, and presents a few examples that call for a deeper engagement between the two fields.

1 Introduction

The recent success of data-driven approaches in NLP has raised important questions as to what role linguistics must now seek to play in further advancing the field. Perhaps, it is also time to pose the same question from the other direction: As to how NLP techniques can help linguists make informed decisions? And how can the advances made in one field be applied to the other?

Although, there has been some work on incorporating NLP techniques for linguistic fieldwork and language documentation (Bird, 2009), the wider use of NLP in linguistic studies is still fairly limited. However, it is possible to deepen the engagement between the two fields in a number of possible areas (as we shall see in the following sections), and gain new insights even during the formulation of linguistic theories and frameworks.

2 Historical Linguistics and Linguistic Typology

Computational techniques have been successfully used to classify languages and to generate phylogenetic trees. This has been tried not just with handcrafted word lists (Atkinson et al., 2005; Atkinson and Gray, 2006; Huelsenbeck et al., 2001) or syntactic data (Barbaçon et al., 2007) but with lists extracted from written corpus with comparable results (Rama and Singh, 2009; Singh and Surana, 2007). These techniques are inspired from the work in computational phylogenetics, which was aimed at constructing evolutionary trees of biological species. Constructing a phylogenetic tree for languages usually requires the calculation of distances between pairs of languages (usually based on word lists). These distances are then given as input to a computational phylogenetic algorithm. Their successful use for languages has opened the possibility of using computational techniques for studying historical linguistics. They have already been used for estimating divergence times of language families (Atkinson et al., 2005). Figure 1 shows a phylogenetic tree created using feature n-grams (Rama and Singh, 2009).

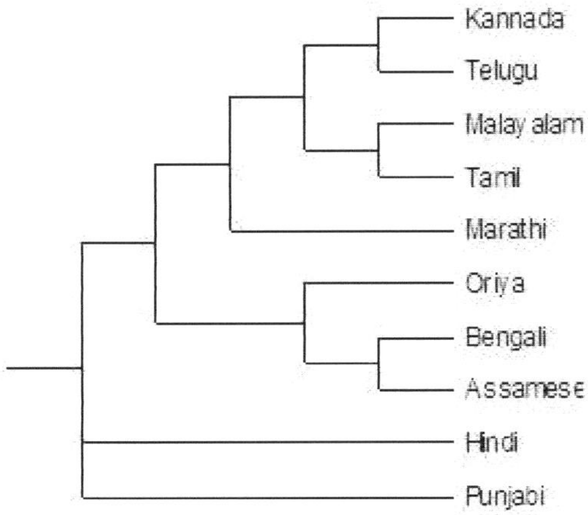

Figure 1: Phylogenetic tree using feature n-grams

Another area for the application of NLP techniques is language typology. For example, linguistic similarity and its estimation can be seen as fundamental ideas in NLP. The systematic study of different kinds of linguistic similarity offers insights towards the theoretical studies of languages (Singh, 2010). In brief, the typology of linguistic similarity for computational purposes is related to linguistic levels (depth), differences among languages (linguality) and linguistic units (granularity). Thus, language can be seen as a system of symbols whose meanings are defined

Proceedings of the 2010 Workshop on NLP and Linguistics: Finding the Common Ground, ACL 2010, pages 18–21,
Uppsala, Sweden, 16 July 2010.

in terms of their estimated similarity and distance with other symbols. Can this, together with what Cognitive Linguists have been studying (Robinson and Ellis, 2008), which also involves linguistic similarity, often directly, have some relevance for linguists?

3 Lexical Correspondence and Linguistic Units

A further case in point is lexical correspondence across languages, which poses a problem for cross-lingual and multilingual applications. To address this and some other issues, a linguistic *unit* that behaves similarly across languages can be conceptualized. Such a unit, may include morphological variation (inflectional and derivational), compounds, multi word expressions etc. as in the Hindi and Telugu examples below:

- Single token content words: *raama, raama* (Ram); *vah, atanu* (he); *vyakti, manishii* (person) etc.
- Nouns with inflections: *bacce, pillalu* (children); *bacce ko, pillalaki* (to the child); *raama se, raamudunundii* (from Rama) etc.
- Verbs with inflections and tense, aspect and modality (TAM) markers: *karnaa-caahiye, cayiyaalii* (should do); *ho sakataa thaa, ayyiyedemo* (could have happened) etc.
- Multi word expressions such as idioms, phrasal verbs and 'frozen expressions': *pahaaD toDanaa* (breaking mountains); *muNha ki khaana* (getting defeated) etc.
- Compounds: *jaati-prathaa* (caste system); *vesh-bhuushaaoN* (dresses); *akkaDaa-ikkaDaa* (here and there) etc.

This unit might, among other things, form the basis of the structure of lexical resources, such that these resources have a direct correspondence across languages. This can further facilitate comparative study of languages (Singh, 2010).

4 Applications

Computational techniques can also be used to design tools and material for language learning and teaching. Here games can play a useful role. Although, a large number of online games are available, most of them do not use the latest language processing techniques. Games can also be used to generate language resources.

The core idea in Human Computation (Von Ahn, 2005) is that computers should do what they do best and that humans seamlessly work with them to do what computers cannot. One of the ways to merge the two is in the form of carefully designed games.

Another insight comes from Machine Translation. More than any other sub-field in NLP, it is the data-driven approaches to machine translation that have proven to be particularly successful over the past few years. We have been exploring various approaches towards hybridization of our rule-based MT system. Building the transfer-grammar of such systems is perhaps one of the most time-intensive tasks that involves careful analysis of test data. However, data driven techniques can come to the aid of linguists in this case. The recent work on automatic acquisition of rules from parallel corpora (Lavie et al., 2004) can help identify a large number of common syntactic transformations across a pair of languages, and help unearth those transformations that might otherwise be missed by a rule-based grammar. They can be further used to prioritize the application of rules based on the observed frequencies of certain syntactic transformations.

5 NLP Tools and Linguistics

NLP techniques draw features from annotated corpora which are a rich linguistic resource. However, these corpora can also be used to extract grammars, which on one hand feed the parser with features (Xia, 2001), and on the other, act as a resource for linguistic studies. For example, in Hindi dependency parsing the use of vibhakti (post-positions) and TAM labels has proven to be particularly useful even in the absence of large amounts of annotated corpora (Ambati et al., 2010). This also helped bring to light those features of the grammar that govern certain structure choices and brought to notice some previously overlooked linguistic constructions. Thus, the result is an iterative process, where both the grammar and the features are refined.

Discourse Processing is another rapidly emerging research area with considerable potential for interaction and collaboration between NLP and Linguistics. In the absence of fully developed theories/frameworks on both sides, focus on synergizing research efforts in the two disciplines (such as devising novel ways to empirically test linguistic hypotheses) from the initial stage itself, can yield a substantially richer account of Discourse.

Linguistic theories are formalized based on observations and abstractions of existing linguistic facts. These theories are then applied to various languages to test their validity. However, languages throw up new problems and issues before theoreticians. Hence, there are always certain phenomena in languages which remain a point of discussion since satisfactory solutions are not available. The facts of a language are accounted for by applying various techniques and methods that are offered by a linguistic framework. For example, syntactic diagnostics have been a fairly reliable method of identifying/classifying construction types in languages. They work fairly well for most cases. But in some cases even these tests fail to classify certain elements. For example, Indian languages show a highly productive use of complex predicates (Butt, 1995; Butt, 2003). However, till date there are no satisfactory methods to decide when a noun verb sequence is a 'complex predicate' and when a 'verb argument' case. To quote an example from our experience while developing a Hindi Tree Bank, annotators had to be provided with guidelines to mark a N V sequence as a complex predicate based on some linguistic tests. However, there are instances when the native speaker/annotator is quite confident of a construction being a complex predicate, even though most syntactic tests might not apply to it.

Although, various theories provide frames to classify linguistic patterns/items but none of them enables us to (at least to my knowledge) handle 'transient/graded' or rather 'evolving' elements. So, as of now it looks like quite an arbitrary/adhoc approach whether to classify something as a complex predicate or not. In the above cited example, the decision is left to the annotator's intuition, since linguists don't agree on the classfication of these elements or on a set of uniform tests either. Can the insights gained from interannotator agreement further help *theory* refine the diagnostics used in these cases? And can NLP techniques or advanced NLP tools come to the aid of linguists here? Perhaps in the form of tools that can (to an extent) help automate the application of syntactic diagnostics over large corpora?

6 Collaborations

Interdisciplinary areas such as Computational Linguistics/NLP need a much broader collaboration between linguists and computer scientists. Experts working within their respective fields tend to be deeply grounded in their approaches towards particular problems. Also, they tend to speak different 'languages'. Therefore, it becomes imperative that efforts be made to bridge the gaps in communication between the two disciplines. This problem is all the more acute in India, since the separation of disciplines happens at a very early stage. Objectives, goals, methods and training are so different that starting a communication line proves to be very difficult. Thus, it is important for those people who have synthesised the knowledge of the two disciplines to a large degree, to take the lead and help establish the initial communication channels. Our own experiences while devising common tagsets for Indian languages, made us realize the need for both linguistic and computational perspectives towards such problems. While a linguist's instinct is to look for exceptions in the grammar (or any formalism), a computer scientist tends to look for rules that can be abstracted away and modeled. However, at the end, both ways of looking at data help us make informed decisions.

Acknowledgements

Many thanks to Dr. Rajeev Sangal, Anil Kumar Singh, Arafat Ahsan, Bharath Ambati, Rafiya Begum, Samar Husain and Sudheer Kolachina for the discussions and inputs.

References

B.R. Ambati, S. Husain, J. Nivre, and R. Sangal. 2010. On the role of morphosyntactic features in Hindi dependency parsing. In *The First Workshop on Statistical Parsing of Morphologically Rich Languages (SPMRL 2010)*, page 94.

QD Atkinson and RD Gray. 2006. How old is the Indo-European language family? Progress or more moths to the flame. *Phylogenetic Methods and the Prehistory of Languages (Forster P, Renfrew C, eds)*, pages 91–109.

Q. Atkinson, G. Nicholls, D. Welch, and R. Gray. 2005. From words to dates: water into wine, mathemagic or phylogenetic inference? *Transactions of the Philological Society*, 103(2):193–219.

S. Bird. 2009. Natural language processing and linguistic fieldwork. *Computational Linguistics*, 35(3):469–474.

M. Butt. 1995. *The structure of complex predicates in Urdu*. Center for the Study of Language and Information.

M. Butt. 2003. The light verb jungle. In *Workshop on Multi-Verb Constructions*. Citeseer.

J.P. Huelsenbeck, F. Ronquist, R. Nielsen, and J.P. Bollback. 2001. Bayesian inference of phylogeny and its impact on evolutionary biology. *Science*, 294(5550):2310–2314.

A. Lavie, K. Probst, E. Peterson, S. Vogel, L. Levin, A. Font-Llitjos, and J. Carbonell. 2004. A trainable transfer-based machine translation approach for languages with limited resources. In *Proceedings of Workshop of the European Association for Machine Translation*. Citeseer.

Taraka Rama and Anil Kumar Singh. 2009. From bag of languages to family trees from noisy corpus. In *Proceedings of the Conference on Recent Advances in Natural Language Processing*, Borovets, Bulgaria.

Peter Robinson and Nick Ellis. 2008. *Handbook of Cognitive Linguistics and Second Language Acquisition*. Routledge, New York and London.

Anil Kumar Singh and Harshit Surana. 2007. Can corpus based measures be used for comparative study of languages? In *Proceedings of the Ninth Meeting of ACL Special Interest Group on Computational Phonology and Morphology*, Prague, Czech Republic. Association for Computational Linguistics.

Anil Kumar Singh. 2010. *Modeling and Application of Linguistic Similarity*. Ph.D. thesis, IIIT, Hyderabad, India.

Luis Von Ahn. 2005. *Human computation*. Ph.D. thesis, Pittsburgh, PA, USA. Adviser-Blum, Manuel.

Fei Xia. 2001. *Automatic Grammar Generation from Two Different Perspectives*. Ph.D. thesis, University of Pennsylvania.

Matching needs and resources: How NLP can help theoretical linguistics

Alexis Dimitriadis
Utrecht institute of Linguistics OTS
a.dimitriadis@uu.nl

Abstract

While some linguistic questions pose challenges that could be met by developing and applying NLP techniques, other problems can best be approached with a blend of old-fashioned linguistic investigation and the use of simple, well-established NLP tools. Unfortunately, this means that the NLP component is too simple to be of interest to the computationally-minded, while existing tools are often difficult for the programming novice to use. For NLP to come to the aid of research in theoretical linguistics, a continuing investment of effort is required to bridge the gap. This investment can be made from both sides.

1 Introduction

Linguistics is in its heart an empirical discipline, and the data management and data analysis techniques of computational linguistics could, in principle, be productively brought to bear on descriptive and theoretical questions. That this does not happen as much as it could is, as I understand it, the point of departure for this colloquium. Instead of focusing on exciting research questions that are crying out for fruitful collaboration between theoretical and computational linguists, I want to examine the broader range of ways that NLP know-how could be put to productive use in the domain of theoretical linguistics, and some of the ways that this could come to happen more.

In brief, I believe that the lack of interaction is not simply due to lack of interest, or lack of information, on both sides. Rather, the goals and needs of computational interests are not always served well by catering to the community of theoretical and descriptive linguists, the so-called "Ordinary Working Linguists" with a minimum of computational skills and (equally important) no direct interest in computational questions.

Such linguists could draw a lot of benefit from boring, old-hat NLP tools that computational linguists take for granted: searchable parsed corpora, tools to search large collections of text or compute lexicostatistics, online questionnaire tools for collecting and analyzing speaker judgements, etc. Computational linguists have ready access to a number of wonderful tools of this sort. In fact these are often the building blocks and resources on which new applications at the forefront of NLP are built: Who would build a text summarization system without access to a large corpus of text to practice on?

But such uses of NLP are too simple to be of interest from the computational standpoint. Searching a huge corpus for particular syntactic structures could be invaluable to a syntactician, but making this possible is not interesting to a computational linguist: it's not research anymore. This should not be taken to suggest, however, that computational linguists ought to become more "altruistic." Creating tools targeted to non-technical linguists, even successful tools, can still have drawbacks in the long run.

2 The Linguist's Search Engine

The Linguist's Search Engine (Resnik et al. 2004) is an example of an application created for the benefit of ordinary, non-technical linguists. It allowed users to search the web for a specified syntactic structure. Out of view of the user, the engine first executed an ordinary word-match web search and then parsed the hits and matched against the search structure. The user interface (a java application) allowed the query term to be graphically constructed and refined ("query by example"). The authors' goal was to create a true web application: Easy to launch from a web browser, and easy to use without lengthy user manuals or a complicated command language. While the user interface was innovative, its linguistic function was not: The ap-

Proceedings of the 2010 Workshop on NLP and Linguistics: Finding the Common Ground, ACL 2010, pages 22–24,
Uppsala, Sweden, 16 July 2010.

plication provided a web interface to a collection of tools that had been assembled to support structured searches. The application stagnated after the end of the project, and ceased working altogether as of April, 2010.

While it was operating, the LSE was used as intended: Resnik et al. report on a number of case studies of users who independently used the search engine to carry out linguistic research. Unfortunately, however, the burden of maintenance turned out to be too great for an application that is of no real continuing interest for a computational linguist.

2.1 The cost of new tools

Complex resources are difficult to create and can be difficult to use. In the world of Language Resources, large corpora are created by the millions of words in various standardized formats, often in conjunction with integrated mega-tools for accessing and managing them. But language resources are geared for institutional clients, can cost a lot of money, and are not acquired or used effectively by individuals without access to dedicated IT support.

At the frontier of NLP, on the other hand, tools don't usually come shrink-wrapped with graphical installers. They often don't come with a graphical interface at all. A new research project may involve a new workflow to be created. Needed corpora will be bought, shared or created as needed. A typical project will involve a jumble of file formats, filters, and workflows that manage text in ad hoc ways until the sought-for result is perfected.

Making such a tool available to someone outside the project, even another computational linguist, is a time-consuming enterprise. Like any complicated body of software, it needs to be documented, encapsulated, and then configured and understood by its new users. This requires a considerable time investment which an NLP lab is willing to undertake, but which is of dubious utility to a theoretical linguist— even one who has the computer skills necessary to undertake it. In brief, the expected amount of use must justify the investment in setting up and learning the system. Tagging, parsing and tree-searching programs are commonplace, but setting up a system for one's own use is a non-trivial exercise. A syntactician looking for a few examples of a rare construction may prefer trial and error on google instead of trying to get a complex system to compile. A syntactician looking for similar data from multiple languages is even less likely to take the plunge, since the benefit derived from a single language is proportionally reduced.

3 Services and interoperability

With the goal of reducing the burden of installing complex resources and getting them to talk to each other, the CLARIN program (Common Language Resources and Technology Infrastructure) is working to establish a cutting edge infrastructure of standards and protocols, which will allow language resources and applications to be utilized remotely, and workflows to be constructed interactively in (hopefully) intuitive ways. The vision is to be able to gain remote access to a language corpus, couple it to a processing application (perhaps an experimental parser using a new syntactic analysis), send the results to yet another application for analysis, etc.

It would be great to have ready access to the tools and resources envisioned for the network. But will it be a platform for development of experimental applications by tomorrow's computational linguists, or will the command line continue to compete with web services as an interface? The answer probably depends on the benefits that CLARIN (and any such framework) will offer to researcher-developers. If adopted, it offers hopes of opening up the computational linguist's toolbox to a wider range of users.

4 Helping ourselves

Wouldn't it be great to have a simple tool for executing simple web searches, converting hits into flat text and compiling the results into a simple corpus? Throw in a tagger, a parser and a search application, and we have the functionality of the Linguist's Search Engine but in several pieces. Tools for most of these tasks are already widely available, but only as part of a complex infrastructure that requires skill and non-trivial time investment to deploy. Other tasks are solved over and over on an ad hoc basis, according to the needs of each NLP project. Until the vision of CLARIN becomes reality, ordinary linguists without access to a team of developers are out of luck.

Still, we need not agree with the perspective (held by Resnik et al. 2005, inter alia) that tools for linguists should be point-and-click and really easy for an untrained user to figure out. Setting the bar that high greatly shrinks the pool of computational linguists willing to write software for the non-technical masses. The life cycle of the Linguist's Search Engine is a case in point.

Instead, linguists should meet the new technology halfway: As Bird (2006) has argued, no integrated tools can be expected to provide the flexibility needed for the creativity of original research. The NLTK (Natural Language Toolkit) is a more flexible alternative: It is a python library providing a high-level scripting environment for interactive linguistic exploration, with a reasonably small amount of technical skill required. Crucially, the NLTK comes with a very accessible book (Bird et al. 2009) that allows an "ordinary working linguist" to learn how to use the system.

The NLTK will still be beyond the reach of linguists unable, or unwilling, to make the necessary time investment. Is this a big problem? I believe that it should be addressed by persuading linguists (especially junior and future ones) of the benefits of achieving a minimal level of computational competence. The availability of more tools that are usable and installable with a moderate investment in training, time and equipment would encourage linguists to make this kind of investment, and would in the long run decrease the support burden for those technology folks who try to make life easier for non-programming linguists. Conversely, computational linguists would hopefully be encouraged to package their programs in a reasonably accessible format if a growing number of potential users is clamoring for them– and if "packaging" need not mean a complete point-and-click interface.

On the subject of command-line tools, I believe that the obstacle is not with the command line per se (anyone can learn to open a terminal window and type a few symbols), but with the powerful and flexible workflows that the command line makes possible. This is the bread and butter of the computational linguist (and of any programmer), and its benefits could belong to descriptive and theoretical linguists as well.

Theoretical linguistics, of course, also has NLP needs that are anything but trivial. At UiL-OTS there are projects underway to model the acquisition of phonotactic constraints; to improve textual entailments (in a linguistically informative way) by taking into account the contribution of lexical meaning; and others. These and other projects can provide challenges that a computational linguist can be happy to tackle. But for theoretical linguistics to fully benefit from NLP, we theoretical linguists need to pick up more of the tools of the computational linguist.

References

Bird, Steven. 2006. "Linguistic Data Management with the Natural Language Toolkit." Plenary talk at the Annual Meeting of the DGfS, Universität Bielefeld.

Bird, Steven, Ewan Klein, and Edward Loper. 2006. *Natural Language Processing with Python: Analyzing Text with the Natural Language Toolkit.* O'Reilly Media.

CLARIN. Common Language Resources and Technology Infrastructure. *http://www.clarin.eu/.*

Resnik, Philip, Aaron Elkiss, Ellen Lau, and Heather Taylor. 2005. "The Web in Theoretical Linguistics Research: Two Case Studies Using the Linguist's Search Engine." *31st Meeting of the Berkeley Linguistics Society,* pp. 265-276.

Grammar-driven versus Data-driven: Which Parsing System is More Affected by Domain Shifts?

Barbara Plank
University of Groningen
The Netherlands
b.plank@rug.nl

Gertjan van Noord
University of Groningen
The Netherlands
G.J.M.van.Noord@rug.nl

Abstract

In the past decade several parsing systems for natural language have emerged, which use different methods and formalisms. For instance, systems that employ a hand-crafted grammar and a statistical disambiguation component versus purely statistical data-driven systems. What they have in common is the lack of portability to new domains: their performance might decrease substantially as the distance between test and training domain increases. Yet, to which degree do they suffer from this problem, i.e. which kind of parsing system is more affected by domain shifts? Intuitively, grammar-driven systems should be less affected by domain changes. To investigate this hypothesis, an empirical investigation on Dutch is carried out. The performance variation of a grammar-driven versus two data-driven systems across domains is evaluated, and a simple measure to quantify domain sensitivity proposed. This will give an estimate of which parsing system is more affected by domain shifts, and thus more in need for adaptation techniques.

1 Introduction

Most modern Natural Language Processing (NLP) systems are subject to the wellknown problem of lack of portability to new domains: there is a substantial drop in their performance when the system gets input from another text domain (Gildea, 2001). This is the problem of *domain adaptation*. Although the problem exists ever since the emergence of supervised Machine Learning, it has started to get attention only in recent years.

Studies on *supervised domain adaptation* (where there are limited amounts of annotated resources in the new domain) have shown that straightforward baselines (e.g. models based on source only, target only, or the union of the data) achieve a relatively high performance level and are "surprisingly difficult to beat" (Daumé III, 2007). In contrast, *semi-supervised adaptation* (i.e. no annotated resources in the new domain) is a much more realistic situation but is clearly also considerably more difficult. Current studies on semi-supervised approaches show very mixed results. Dredze et al. (2007) report on "frustrating" results on the CoNLL 2007 semi-supervised adaptation task for dependency parsing, i.e. "no team was able to improve target domain performance substantially over a state-of-the-art baseline". On the other hand, there have been positive results as well. For instance, McClosky et al. (2006) improved a statistical parser by self-training. Structural Correspondence Learning (Blitzer et al., 2006) was effective for PoS tagging and Sentiment Analysis (Blitzer et al., 2006; Blitzer et al., 2007), while only modest gains were obtained for structured output tasks like parsing.

For parsing, most previous work on domain adaptation has focused on *data-driven* systems (Gildea, 2001; McClosky et al., 2006; Dredze et al., 2007), i.e. systems employing (constituent or dependency based) treebank grammars. Only few studies examined the adaptation of *grammar-based* systems (Hara et al., 2005; Plank and van Noord, 2008), i.e. systems employing a hand-crafted grammar with a statistical disambiguation component. This may be motivated by the fact that potential gains for this task are inherently bound by the grammar. Yet, domain adaptation poses a challenge for both kinds of parsing systems. But to what extent do these different kinds of systems suffer from the problem? We test the hypothesis that grammar-driven systems are less affected by domain changes. We empirically investigate this in a case-study on Dutch.

Proceedings of the 2010 Workshop on NLP and Linguistics: Finding the Common Ground, ACL 2010, pages 25–33,
Uppsala, Sweden, 16 July 2010.

2 Related work

Most previous work has focused on a single parsing system in isolation (Gildea, 2001; Hara et al., 2005; McClosky et al., 2006). However, there is an observable trend towards combining different parsing systems to exploit complementary strengths. For instance, Nivre and McDonald (2008) combine two data-driven systems to improve dependency accuracy. Similarly, two studies successfully combined grammar-based and data-driven systems: Sagae et al. (2007) incorporate data-driven dependencies as soft-constraint in a HPSG-based system for parsing the Wallstreet Journal. In the same spirit (but the other direction), Zhang and Wang (2009) use a deep-grammar based backbone to improve data-driven parsing accuracy. They incorporate features from the grammar-based backbone into the data-driven system to achieve better generalization across domains. This is the work most closest to ours.

However, which kind of system (hand-crafted versus purely statistical) is more affected by the domain, and thus more sensitive to domain shifts? To the best of our knowledge, no study has yet addressed this issue. We thus assess the performance variation of three dependency parsing systems for Dutch across domains, and propose a simple measure to quantify domain sensitivity.

3 Parsing Systems

The parsing systems used in this study are: a grammar-based system for Dutch (Alpino) and two data-driven systems (MST and Malt), all described next.

(1) Alpino is a parser for Dutch which has been developed over the last ten years, on the basis of a domain-specific HPSG-grammar that was used in the OVIS spoken dialogue system. The OVIS parser was shown to out-perform a statistical (DOP) parser, in a contrastive formal evaluation (van Zanten et al., 1999). In the ten years after this evaluation, the system has developed into a generic parser for Dutch. Alpino consists of more than 800 grammar rules in the tradition of HPSG, and a large hand-crafted lexicon. It produces dependency structures as ouput, where more than a single head per token is allowed. For words that are not in the lexicon, the system applies a large variety of unknown word heuristics (van Noord, 2006), which deal with number-like expressions, compounds, proper names, etc. Coverage of the grammar and lexicon has been extended over the years by paying careful attention to the results of parsing large corpora, by means of error mining techniques (van Noord, 2004; de Kok et al., 2009).

Lexical ambiguity is reduced by means of a POS-tagger, described in (Prins and van Noord, 2003). This POS-tagger is trained on large amounts of parser output, and removes unlikely lexical categories. Some amount of lexical ambiguity remains. A left-corner parser constructs a parse-forest for an input sentence. Based on large amounts of parsed data, the parser considers only promising parse step sequences, by filtering out sequences of parse steps which were not previously used to construct a best parse for a given sentence. The parse step filter improves efficiency considerably (van Noord, 2009).

A best-first beam-search algorithm retrieves the best parse(s) from that forest by consulting a Maximum Entropy disambiguation component. Features for the disambiguation component include non-local features. For instance, there are features that can be used to learn a preference for local extraction over long-distance extraction, and a preference for subject fronting rather than direct object fronting, and a preference for certain types of orderings in the "mittelfeld" of a Dutch sentence. The various features that we use for disambiguation, as well as the best-first algorithm is described in (van Noord, 2006). The model now also contains features which implement selection restrictions, trained on the basis of large parsed corpora (van Noord, 2007). The maximum entropy disambiguation component is trained on the Alpino treebank, described below.

To illustrate the role of the disambiguation component, we provide some results for the first 536 sentences of one of the folds of the training data (of course, the model used in this experiment is trained on the remaining folds of training data). In this setup, the POS-tagger and parse step filter already filter out many, presumably bad, parses. This table indicates that a very large amount of parses can be constructed for some sentences. Furthermore, the maximum entropy disambiguation component does a good job in selecting good parses from those. Accuracy is given here in terms of f-score of named dependencies.

sents	parses	oracle	arbitrary	model
536	45011	95.74	76.56	89.39

(2) *MST Parser* (McDonald et al., 2005) is a

data-driven graph-based dependency parser. The system couples a minimum spanning tree search procedure with a separate second stage classifier to label the dependency edges.

(3) *MALT Parser* (Nivre et al., 2007) is a data-driven transition-based dependency parser. Malt parser uses SVMs to learn a classifier that predicts the next parsing action. Instances represent parser configurations and the label to predict determines the next parser action.

Both data-driven parsers (MST and Malt) are thus not specific for the Dutch Language, however, they can be trained on a variety of languages given that the training corpus complies with the column-based format introduced in the 2006 CoNLL shared task (Buchholz and Marsi, 2006). Additionally, both parsers implement projective and non-projective parsing algorithms, where the latter will be used in our experiments on the relatively free word order language Dutch. Despite that, we train the data-driven parsers using their default settings (e.g. first order features for MST, SVM with polynomial kernel for Malt).

4 Datasets and experimental setup

The source domain on which all parsers are trained is cdb, the Alpino Treebank (van Noord, 2006). For our cross-domain evaluation, we consider Wikipedia and DPC (Dutch Parallel Corpus) as target data. All datasets are described next.

Source: Cdb The cdb (Alpino Treebank) consists of 140,000 words (7,136 sentences) from the Eindhoven corpus (newspaper text). It is a collection of text fragments from 6 Dutch newspapers. The collection has been annotated according to the guidelines of CGN (Oostdijk, 2000) and stored in XML format. It is the standard treebank used to train the disambiguation component of the Alpino parser. Note that cdb is a subset of the training corpus used in the CoNLL 2006 shared task (Buchholz and Marsi, 2006). The CoNLL training data additionally contained a mix of non-newspaper text,[1] which we exclude here on purpose to keep a clean baseline.

Target: Wikipedia and DPC We use the Wikipedia and DPC subpart of the LASSY corpus[2] as target domains. These corpora contain several domains, e.g. sports, locations, science. On overview of the corpora is given in Table 1. Note that both consist of hand-corrected data labeled by Alpino, thus all domains employ the same annotation scheme. This might introduce a slight bias towards Alpino, however it has the advantage that all domains employ the same annotation scheme – which was the major source of error in the CoNLL task on domain adaptation (Dredze et al., 2007).

Wikipedia	Example articles	#a	#w	ASL
LOC (location)	Belgium, Antwerp (city)	31	25259	11.5
KUN (arts)	Tervuren school	11	17073	17.1
POL (politics)	Belgium elections 2003	16	15107	15.4
SPO (sports)	Kim Clijsters	9	9713	11.1
HIS (history)	History of Belgium	3	8396	17.9
BUS (business)	Belgium Labour Federation	9	4440	11.0
NOB (nobility)	Albert II	6	4179	15.1
COM (comics)	Suske and Wiske	3	4000	10.5
MUS (music)	Sandra Kim, Urbanus	3	1296	14.6
HOL (holidays)	Flemish Community Day	4	524	12.2
Total		**95**	**89987**	**13.4**

DPC	Description/Example	#a	#words	ASL
Science	medicine, oeanography	69	60787	19.2
Institutions	political speeches	21	28646	16.1
Communication	ICT/Internet	29	26640	17.5
Welfare state	pensions	22	20198	17.9
Culture	darwinism	11	16237	20.5
Economy	inflation	9	14722	18.5
Education	education in Flancers	2	11980	16.3
Home affairs	presentation (Brussel)	1	9340	17.3
Foreign affairs	European Union	7	9007	24.2
Environment	threats/nature	6	8534	20.4
Finance	banks (education banker)	6	6127	22.3
Leisure	various (drugscandal)	2	2843	20.3
Consumption	toys from China	1	1310	22.6
Total		**186**	**216371**	**18.5**

Table 1: Overview Wikipedia and DPC corpus (#a articles, #w words, ASL average sentence length)

CoNLL2006 This is the testfile for Dutch that was used in the CoNLL 2006 shared task on multilingual dependency parsing. The file consists of 386 sentences from an institutional brochure (about youth healthcare). We use this file to check our data-driven models against state-of-the-art.

Alpino to CoNLL format In order to train the MST and Malt parser and evaluate it on the various Wikipedia and DPC articles, we needed to convert the Alpino Treebank format into the tabular CoNLL format. To this end, we adapted the treebank conversion software developed by Erwin Marsi for the CoNLL 2006 shared task on multilingual dependency parsing. Instead of using the PoS tagger and tagset used in the shared task (to which we did not have access to), we replaced the PoS tags with more fine-grained tags obtained by

[1]Namely, a large amount of questions (from CLEF, roughly 4k sentences) and hand-crafted sentences used during the development of the grammar (1.5k).

[2]LASSY (Large Scale Syntactic Annotation of written Dutch), ongoing project. Corpus version 17905, obtained from `http://www.let.rug.nl/vannoord/Lassy/corpus/`

parsing the data with the Alpino parser.[3] At testing time, the data-driven parsers are given PoS tagged input, while Alpino gets plain sentences.

Evaluation In all experiments, unless otherwise specified, performance is measured as Labeled Attachment Score (LAS), the percentage of tokens with the correct dependency edge and label. To compute LAS, we use the CoNLL 2007 evaluation script[4] with punctuation tokens excluded from scoring (as was the default setting in CoNLL 2006). We thus evaluate all parsers using the same evaluation metric. Note that the standard metric for Alpino would be a variant of LAS, which allows for a discrepancy between expected and returned dependencies. Such a discrepancy can occur, for instance, because the syntactic annotation of Alpino allows words to be dependent on more than a single head ('secondary edges') (van Noord, 2006). However, such edges are ignored in the CoNLL format; just a single head per token is allowed. Furthermore, there is another simplification. As the Dutch tagger used in the CoNLL 2006 shared task did not have the concept of multiwords, the organizers chose to treat them as a single token (Buchholz and Marsi, 2006). We here follow the CoNLL 2006 task setup. To determine whether results are significant, we us the *Approximate Randomization Test* (see Yeh (2000)) with 1000 random shuffles.

5 Domain sensitivity

The problem of domain dependence poses a challenge for both kinds of parsing systems, data-driven and grammar-driven. However, to what extent? Which kind of parsing system is more affected by domain shifts? We may rephrase our question as: Which parsing system is more robust to different input texts? To answer this question, we will examine the robustness of the different parsing systems in terms of variation of accuracy on a variety of domains.

A measure of domain sensitivity Given a parsing system (p) trained on some source domain and evaluated on a set of N target domains, the most intuitive measure would be to simply calculate mean (μ) and standard deviation (sd) of the performance on the target domains:

LAS_p^i = accuracy of parser p on target domain i

$$\mu_p^{target} = \frac{\sum_{i=1}^{N} LAS_p^i}{N}, sd_p^{target} = \sqrt{\frac{\sum_{i=1}^{N}(LAS_p^i - \mu_p^{target})^2}{N-1}}$$

However, standard deviation is highly influenced by outliers. Furthermore, this measure does not take the source domain performance (baseline) into consideration nor the size of the target domain itself. We thus propose to measure the domain sensitivity of a system, i.e. its *average domain variation* (adv), as weighted average difference from the baseline (source) mean, where weights represents the size of the various domains:

$$adv = \frac{\sum_{i=1}^{N} w^i * \Delta_p^i}{\sum_{i=1}^{N} w^i}, \text{ with}$$

$$\Delta_p^i = LAS_p^i - LAS_p^{baseline} \text{ and } w^i = \frac{size(w^i)}{\sum_{i=1}^{N} size(w^i)}$$

In more detail, we measure *average domain variation* (adv) relative to the baseline (source domain) performance by considering non-squared differences from the out-of-domain mean and weigh it by domain size. The adv measure can thus take on positive or negative values. Intuitively, it will indicate the average weighted gain or loss in performance, relative to the source domain. As alternative, we may want to just calculate a straight, unweighted average: $uadv = \sum_{i=1}^{N} \Delta_p^i / N$. However, this assumes that domains have a representative size, and a threshold might be needed to disregard domains that are presumably too small.

We will use adv in the empirical result section to evaluate the domain sensitivity of the parsers, where $size$ will be measured in terms of number of words. We additionally provide values for the unweighted version using domains with at least 4000 words (cf. Table 1).

6 Empirical results

First of all, we performed several sanity checks. We trained the MST parser on the entire original CoNLL training data as well as the cdb subpart only, and evaluated it on the original CoNLL test data. As shown in Table 2 (row 1-2) the accuracies of both models falls slightly below state-of-the-art performance (row 5), most probably due to the fact that we used standard parsing settings (e.g.

[3] As discussed later (Section 6, cf. Table 2), using Alpino tags actually improves the performance of the data-driven parsers. We could perform this check as we recently got access to the tagger and tagset used in the CoNLL shared task (Mbt with wotan tagset; thanks to Erwin Marsi).

[4] http://nextens.uvt.nl/depparse-wiki/SoftwarePage

no second-order features for MST). More importantly, there was basically no difference in performance when trained on the entire data or cdb only.

Model	LAS	UAS
MST (original CoNLL)	78.35	82.89
MST (original CoNLL, cdb subpart)	78.37	82.71
MST (cdb retagged with Alpino)	82.14	85.51
Malt (cdb retagged with Alpino)	80.64	82.66
MST (Nivre and McDonald, 2008)	79.19	83.6
Malt (Nivre and McDonald, 2008)	78.59	n/a
MST (cdb retagged with Mbt)	78.73	82.66
Malt (cdb retagged with Mbt)	75.34	78.29

Table 2: Performance of data-driven parsers versus state-of-the-art on the CoNLL 2006 testset (in Labeled/Unlabeled Attachment Score).

We then trained the MST and Malt parser on the cdb corpus converted into the retagged CoNLL format, and tested on CoNLL 2006 test data (also retagged with Alpino). As seen in Table 2, by using Alpino tags the performance level significantly improves (with $p < 0.002$ using Approximate Randomization Test with 1000 iterations). This increase in performance can be attributed to two sources: (a) improvements in the Alpino treebank itself over the course of the years, and (b) the more fine-grained PoS tagset obtained by parsing the data with the deep grammar. To examine the contribution of each source, we trained an additional MST model on the cdb data but tagged with the same tagger as in the CoNLL shared task (Mbt, cf. Table 2 last row): the results show that the major source of improvement actually comes from using the more fine-grained Alpino tags ($78.73 \rightarrow 82.14 = +3.41$ LAS), rather than the changes in the treebank ($78.37 \rightarrow 78.73 = +0.36$ LAS). Thus, despite the rather limited training data and use of standard training settings, we are in line with, and actually above, current results of data-driven parsing for Dutch.

Baselines To establish our baselines, we perform 5-fold cross validation for each parser on the source domain (cdb corpus, newspaper text). The baselines for each parser are given in Table 3. The grammar-driven parser Alpino achieves a baseline that is significantly higher (90.75% LAS) compared to the baselines of the data-driven systems (around 80-83% LAS).

Cross-domain results As our goal is to assess performance variation across domains, we evaluate each parser on the Wikipedia and DPC corpora

Model	Alpino	MST	Malt
Baseline (LAS)	90.76	83.63	79.95
Baseline (UAS)	92.47	88.12	83.31

Table 3: Baseline (5-fold cross-validation). All differences are significant at $p < 0.001$.

that cover a variety of domains (described in Table 1). Figure 1 and Figure 2 summarizes the results for each corpus, respectively. In more detail, the figures depict for each parser the baseline performance as given in Table 3 (straight lines) and the performance on every domain (bars). Note that domains are ordered by size (number of words), so that the largest domains appear as bars on the left. Similar graphs come up if we replace labeled attachment score with its unlabeled variant.

Figure 1 depicts parser performance on the Wikipedia domains with respect to the source domain baseline. The figure indicates that the grammar-driven parser does not suffer much from domain shifts. Its performance falls even above baseline for several Wikipedia domains. In contrast, the MST parser suffers the most from the domain changes; on most domains a substantial performance drop can be observed. The transition-based parser scores on average significantly lower than the graph-based counterpart and Alpino, but seems to be less affected by the domain shifts.

We can summarize this findings by our proposed average domain variation measure (unweighted scores are given in the Figure): On average (over all Wikipedia domains), Alpino suffers the least ($adv = +0.81$), followed by Malt ($+0.59$) and MST (-2.2), which on average loses 2.2 absolute LAS. Thus, the graph-based data-driven dependency parser MST suffers the most.

We evaluate the parsers also on the more varied DPC corpus. It contains a broader set of domains, amongst others science texts (medical texts from the European Medicines Agency as well as texts about oceanography) and articles with more technical vocabulary (Communication, i.e. Internet/ICT texts). The results are depicted in Figure 2. Both Malt ($adv = 0.4$) and Alpino ($adv = 0.22$) achieve on average a gain over the baseline, with this time Malt being slightly less domain affected than Alpino (most probably because Malt scores above average on the more influential/larger domains). Nevertheless, Alpino's performance level is significantly higher compared to both data-driven counterparts. The graph-based data-driven

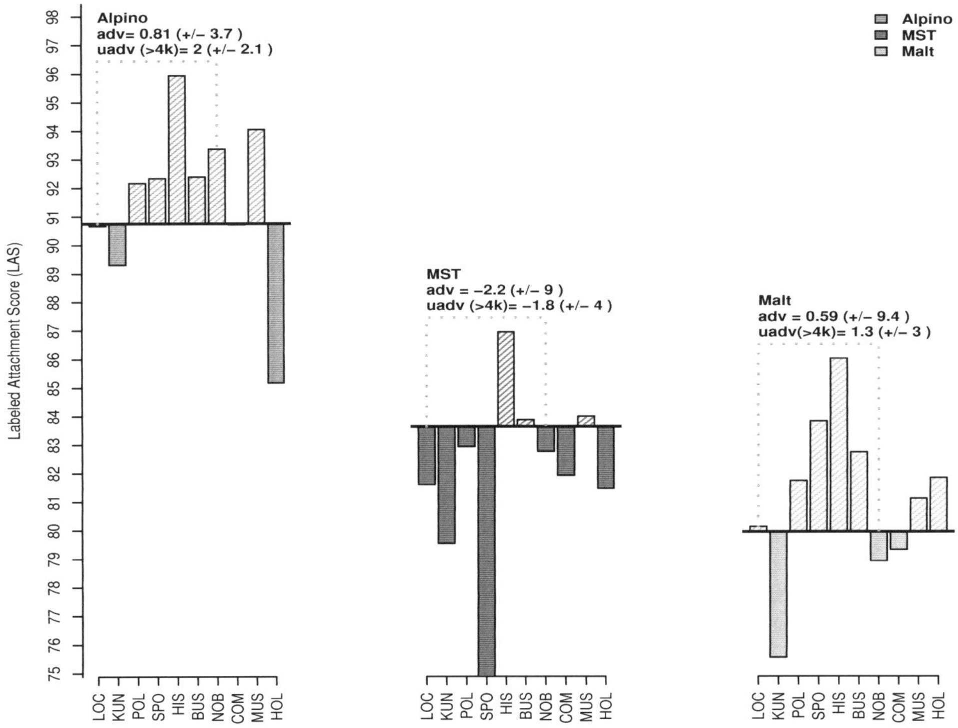

Figure 1: Performance on Wikipedia domains with respect to the source baseline (newspaper text) including average domain variation (adv) score and its unweighted alternative (uadv). Domains are ordered by size (largest on left). Full-colored bars indicate domains where performance lies below the baseline.

parser MST is the most domain-sensitive parser also on DPC ($adv = -0.27$).

In contrast, if we would take only the deviation on the target domains into consideration (without considering the baseline, cf. Section 5), we would get a completely opposite ranking on DPC, where the Malt parser would actually be considered the most domain-sensitive (here higher sd means higher sensitivity): Malt ($sd = 1.20$), MST ($sd = 1.14$), Alpino ($sd = 1.05$). However, by looking at Figure 2, intuitively, MST suffers more from the domain shifts than Malt, as most bars lie below the baseline. Moreover, the standard deviation measure neither gives a sense of whether the parser on average suffers a loss or gain over the new domains, nor incorporates the information of domain size. We thus believe our proposed average domain variation is a better suited measure.

To check whether the differences in performance variation are statistically significant, we performed an Approximate Randomization Test over the performance differences (deltas) on the 23 domains (DPC and Wikipedia). The results show that the difference between Alpino and MST is significant. The same goes for the difference between MST and Malt. Thus Alpino is significantly more robust than MST. However, the difference between Alpino and Malt is not significant. These findings hold for differences measured in both labeled and unlabeled attachments scores. Furthermore, all differences in absolute performance across domains are significant.

To summarize, our empirical evaluation shows that the grammar-driven system Alpino is rather robust across domains. It is the best performing system and it is significantly more robust than MST. In constrast, the transition-based parser Malt scores the lowest across all domains, but its variation turned out not to be different from Alpino. Over all domains, MST is the most domain-sensitive parser.

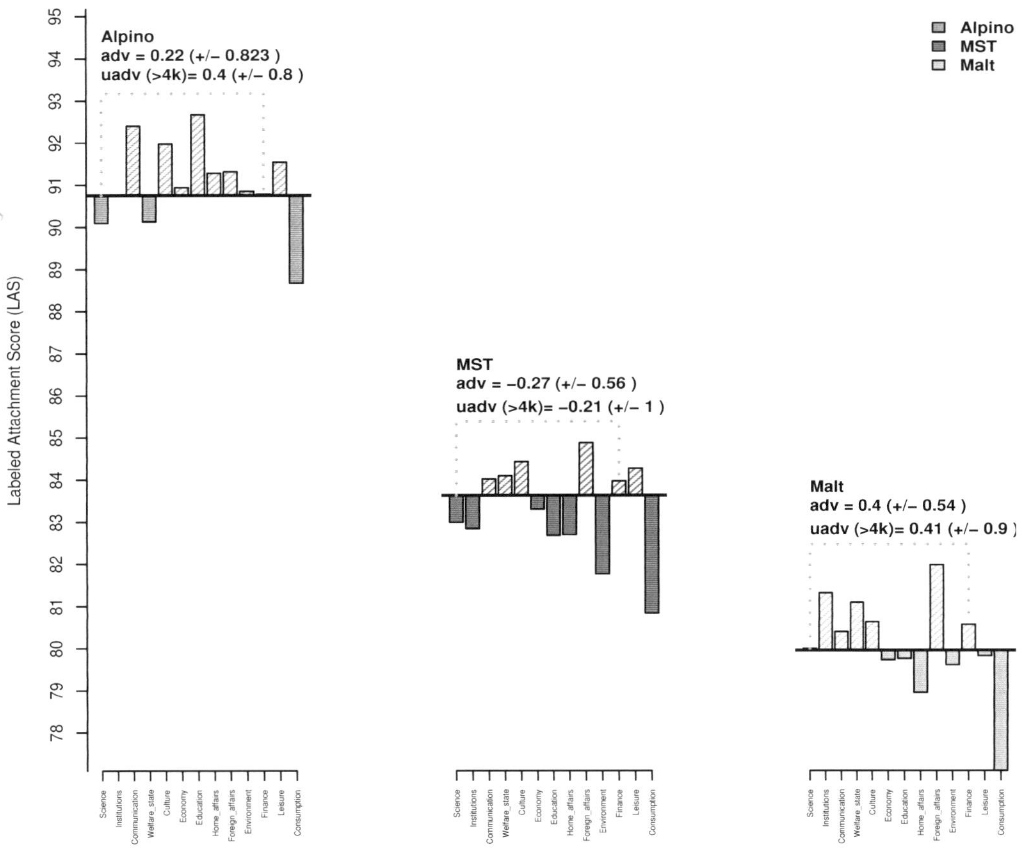

Figure 2: Performance on DPC domains with respect to the source baseline (newspaper text).

Excursion: Lexical information Both kinds of parsing systems rely on lexical information (words/stems) when learning their parsing (or parse disambiguation) model. However, how much influence does lexical information have?

To examine this issue, we retrain all parsing systems by excluding lexical information. As all parsing systems rely on a feature-based representation, we remove all feature templates that include words and thus train models on a reduced feature space (original versus reduced space: Alpino 24k/7k features; MST 14M/1.9M features; Malt 17/13 templates). The result of evaluating the unlexicaled models on Wikipedia are shown in Figure 3. Clearly, performance drops for for all parsers in all domains. However, for the data-driven parsers to a much higher degree. For instance, MST loses on average 11 absolute points in performance ($adv = -11$) and scores below baseline on all Wikipedia domains. In contrast, the grammar-driven parser Alpino suffers far less, still scores above baseline on some domains.[5] The Malt parser lies somewhere in between, also suffers from the missing lexical information, but to a lesser degree than the graph-based parser MST.

7 Conclusions and Future work

We examined a grammar-based system coupled with a statistical disambiguation component (Alpino) and two data-driven statistical parsing systems (MST and Malt) for dependency parsing of Dutch. By looking at the performance variation across a large variety of domains, we addressed the question of how sensitive the parsing systems are to the text domain. This, to gauge which kind

[5]Note that the parser has still access to its lexicon here; for now we removed lexicalized features from the trainable part of Alpino, the statistical disambiguation component.

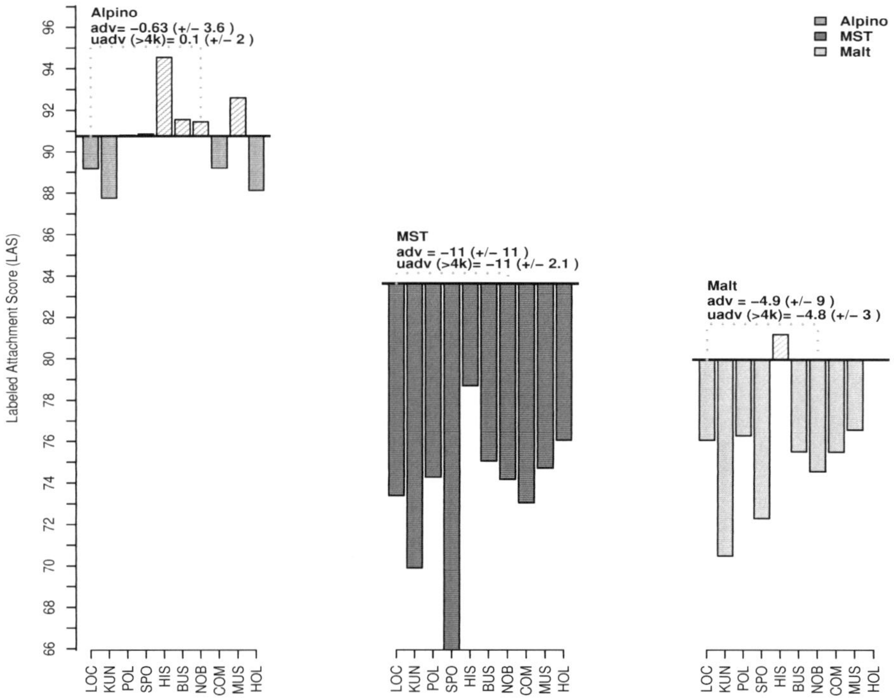

Figure 3: Performance of unlexical parsers on Wikipedia domains with respect to the source baseline.

of system (data-driven versus grammar-driven) is more affected by domain shifts, and thus more in need for adaptation techniques. We also proposed a simple measure to quantify domain sensitivity.

The results show that the grammar-based system Alpino is the best performing system, and it is robust across domains. In contrast, MST, the graph-based approach to data-driven parsing is the most domain-sensitive parser. The results for Malt indicate that its variation across domains is limited, but this parser is outperformed by both other systems on all domains. In general, data-driven systems heavily rely on the training data to estimate their models. This becomes apparent when we exclude lexical information from the training process, which results in a substantial performance drop for the data-driven systems, MST and Malt. The grammar-driven model was more robust against the missing lexical information. Grammar-driven systems try to encode domain independent linguistic knowledge, but usually suffer from coverage problems. The Alpino parser successfully implements a set of unknown word heuristics and a partial parsing strategy (in case no full parse can be found) to overcome this problem. This makes the system rather robust across domains, and, as shown in this study, significantly more robust than MST. This is not to say that domain dependence does not consitute a problem for grammar-driven parsers at all. As also noted by Zhang and Wang (2009), the disambiguation component and lexical coverage of grammar-based systems are still domain-dependent. Thus, domain dependence is a problem for both types of parsing systems, though, as shown in this study, to a lesser extent for the grammar-based system Alpino. Of course, these results are specific for Dutch; however, it's a first step. As the proposed methods are indepedent of language and parsing system, they can be applied to another system or language.

In future, we would like to (a) perform an error analysis (e.g. why for some domains the parsers outperform their baseline; what are typical in-domain and out-domain errors), (a) examine why there is such a difference in performance variation between Malt and MST, and (c) investigate what part(s) of the Alpino parser are responsible for the differences with the data-driven parsers.

References

John Blitzer, Ryan McDonald, and Fernando Pereira. 2006. Domain adaptation with structural correspondence learning. In *Conference on Empirical Methods in Natural Language Processing*, Sydney.

John Blitzer, Mark Dredze, and Fernando Pereira. 2007. Biographies, bollywood, boom-boxes and blenders: Domain adaptation for sentiment classification. In *ACL*, Prague, Czech Republic.

Sabine Buchholz and Erwin Marsi. 2006. Conll-x shared task on multilingual dependency parsing. In *In Proc. of CoNLL*, pages 149–164.

Hal Daumé III. 2007. Frustratingly easy domain adaptation. In *ACL*, Prague, Czech Republic.

Daniël de Kok, Jianqiang Ma, and Gertjan van Noord. 2009. A generalized method for iterative error mining in parsing results. In *Proceedings of the 2009 Workshop on Grammar Engineering Across Frameworks (GEAF 2009)*, pages 71–79, Suntec, Singapore, August.

Mark Dredze, John Blitzer, Pratha Pratim Talukdar, Kuzman Ganchev, Joao Graca, and Fernando Pereira. 2007. Frustratingly hard domain adaptation for parsing. In *Proceedings of the CoNLL Shared Task Session*, Prague, Czech Republic.

Daniel Gildea. 2001. Corpus variation and parser performance. In *Proceedings of the 2001 Conference on Empirical Methods in Natural Language Processing (EMNLP)*.

Tadayoshi Hara, Miyao Yusuke, and Jun'ichi Tsujii. 2005. Adapting a probabilistic disambiguation model of an hpsg parser to a new domain. In *Proceedings of the International Joint Conference on Natural Language Processing*.

David McClosky, Eugene Charniak, and Mark Johnson. 2006. Effective self-training for parsing. In *Proceedings of the Human Language Technology Conference of the NAACL, Main Conference*, pages 152–159, New York City.

Ryan McDonald, Fernando Pereira, Kiril Ribarov, and Jan Hajič. 2005. Non-projective dependency parsing using spanning tree algorithms. In *In Proceedings of Human Language Technology Conference and Conference on Empirical Methods in Natural Language Processing*, pages 523–530.

Joakim Nivre and Ryan McDonald. 2008. Integrating graph-based and transition-based dependency parsers. In *Proceedings of ACL-08: HLT*, pages 950–958, Columbus, Ohio, June.

Joakim Nivre, Johan Hall, Jens Nilsson, Atanas Chanev, Gülsen Eryigit, Sandra Kübler, Svetoslav Marinov, and Erwin Marsi. 2007. Maltparser: A language-independent system for data-driven dependency parsing. *Natural Language Engineering*, 13:95–135.

Nelleke Oostdijk. 2000. The Spoken Dutch Corpus: Overview and first evaluation. In *Proceedings of LREC*, pages 887–894.

Barbara Plank and Gertjan van Noord. 2008. Exploring an auxiliary distribution based approach to domain adaptation of a syntactic disambiguation model. In *Proceedings of the Workshop on Cross-Framework and Cross-Domain Parser Evaluation (PE)*, Manchester, August.

Robbert Prins and Gertjan van Noord. 2003. Reinforcing parser preferences through tagging. *Traitement Automatique des Langues*, 44(3):121–139.

Kenji Sagae, Yusuke Miyao, and Jun'ichi Tsujii. 2007. Hpsg parsing with shallow dependency constraints. In *Proceedings of the 45th Annual Meeting of the Association of Computational Linguistics*, pages 624–631, Prague, Czech Republic, June.

Gertjan van Noord. 2004. Error mining for wide-coverage grammar engineering. In *ACL2004*, Barcelona. ACL.

Gertjan van Noord. 2006. **At Last Parsing Is Now Operational**. In *TALN 2006 Verbum Ex Machina, Actes De La 13e Conference sur Le Traitement Automatique des Langues naturelles*, pages 20–42, Leuven.

Gertjan van Noord. 2007. Using self-trained bilexical preferences to improve disambiguation accuracy. In *Proceedings of the International Workshop on Parsing Technology (IWPT)*, ACL 2007 Workshop, pages 1–10, Prague. ACL.

Gertjan van Noord. 2009. Learning efficient parsing. In *EACL 2009, The 12th Conference of the European Chapter of the Association for Computational Linguistics*, pages 817–825, Athens, Greece.

Gert Veldhuijzen van Zanten, Gosse Bouma, Khalil Sima'an, Gertjan van Noord, and Remko Bonnema. 1999. Evaluation of the NLP components of the OVIS2 spoken dialogue system. In Frank van Eynde, Ineke Schuurman, and Ness Schelkens, editors, *Computational Linguistics in the Netherlands 1998*, pages 213–229. Rodopi Amsterdam.

Alexander Yeh. 2000. More accurate tests for the statistical significance of result differences. In *ACL*, pages 947–953, Morristown, NJ, USA.

Yi Zhang and Rui Wang. 2009. Cross-domain dependency parsing using a deep linguistic grammar. In *Proceedings of the Joint Conference of the 47th Annual Meeting of the ACL and the 4th International Joint Conference on Natural Language Processing of the AFNLP*, pages 378–386, Suntec, Singapore, August.

A Cross-Lingual Induction Technique for German Adverbial Participles

Sina Zarrieß **Aoife Cahill** **Jonas Kuhn** **Christian Rohrer**
Institut für Maschinelle Sprachverarbeitung (IMS)
University of Stuttgart
Stuttgart, Germany
{zarriesa,cahillae,jonas.kuhn,rohrer}@ims.uni-stuttgart.de

Abstract

We provide a detailed comparison of strategies for implementing medium-to-low frequency phenomena such as German adverbial participles in a broad-coverage, rule-based parsing system. We show that allowing for general adverb conversion of participles in the German LFG grammar seriously affects its overall performance, due to increased spurious ambiguity. As a solution, we present a corpus-based cross-lingual induction technique that detects adverbially used participles in parallel text. In a grammar-based evaluation, we show that the automatically induced resource appropriately restricts the adverb conversion to a limited class of participles, and improves parsing quantitatively as well as qualitatively.

1 Introduction

In German, past perfect participles are ambiguous with respect to their morphosyntactic category. As in other languages, they can be used as part of the verbal complex (example (1-a)) or as adjectives (example (1-b)). Since German adjectives can generally undergo conversion into adverbs, participles can also be used adverbially (example (1-c)). All three participle forms in (1) are morphologically identical.

(1) a. Das Experiment hat ihn **begeistert**.
'The experiment has enthused him.'
b. Er scheint von dem Experiment **begeistert**.
'He seems enthusiastic about the experiment.'
c. Er hat **begeistert** experimentiert.
'He has experimented in an enthusiastic way' or:
'He was enthusiastic when he experimented.'

This paper adresses the question of how to deal with medium-to-low frequency phenomena such as adverbial participles in a broad-coverage, rule-based parsing system. In order to account for sentences like (1-c), an intuitive approach would be to generally allow for adverb conversion of participles in the grammar. However, on the basis of the German LFG grammar (Rohrer and Forst, 2006), we show that such a rule can have a strong negative on the overall performance of the parsing system, despite the fact that it produces the desired syntactic and semantic analysis for specific sentences.

This trade-off between large-scale, statistical and theoretically precise coverage is often encountered in engineering broad-coverage and, at the same time, linguistically motivated parsing systems: adding the analysis for a specific phenomenon does not necessarily improve the overall quality of the system since the rule might overgenerate and interact with completely different phenomena in unpredicted ways.

In principle, there are two ways of dealing with such an overgeneration problem in a grammar-based framework: First, one could hand-craft word lists or other linguistic constraints that restrict the adverb conversion to a certain set of participles. Second, one could try to mine corpora for this particular type of adverbs and integrate this automatically induced knowledge into the grammar (i.e. by means of pre-tagged input, word lists, etc.). In the case of adverbial participles, both ways are prone with difficulties. To our knowledge, there has not been much theoretical work on the linguistic properties of the participle adverb conversion. Moreover, since the distinction between (predicative) adjectives and adverbs is theoretically hard to establish, the standard tag set for German and, in consequence, annotated corpora for German do not explicitly capture this phenomenon. Thus, available statistical taggers and parsers for German usually conflate the syntactic structures underlying (1-b) and (1-c).

In this paper, we present a corpus-based approach to restricting the overgenerating adverb conversion for participles in German, exploiting

Proceedings of the 2010 Workshop on NLP and Linguistics: Finding the Common Ground, ACL 2010, pages 34–42,
Uppsala, Sweden, 16 July 2010.

parallel corpora and cross-lingual NLP induction techniques. Since adverbs are often overtly marked in other languages (i.e. the *ly*-suffix in English), adverbial participles can be straightforwadly detected on word-aligned parallel text. We describe the ingretation of the automatically induced resource of adverbial participles into the German LFG, and provide a detailed evaluation of its effect on the grammar, see Section 5.

While the use of parallel resources is rather familiar in a wide range of NLP domains, such as statistical machine translation (Koehn, 2005) or annotation projection (Yarowsky et al., 2001), our work shows that they can be exploited for very specific problems that arise in deep linguistic analysis (see Section 4). In this way, high-precision, data-oriented induction techniques can clearly improve rule-based system development through combining the benefits of high empirical accuracy and little manual effort.

2 A Broad-Coverage LFG for German

Lexical Functional Grammar (LFG) (Bresnan, 2000) is a constraint-based theory of grammar. It posits two levels of representation, c(onstituent)-structure and f(unctional)- structure. C-structure is represented by contextfree phrase-structure trees, and captures surface grammatical configurations. F-structures approximate basic predicate-argument and adjunct structures.

The experiments reported in this paper use the German LFG grammar constructed as part of the ParGram project (Butt et al., 2002). The grammar is implemented in the XLE, a grammar development environment which includes a very efficient LFG parser. Within the spectrum of appraoches to natural language parsing, XLE can be considered a hybrid system combining a hand-crafted grammar with a number of automatic ambiguity management techniques: (i) c-structure pruning where, based on information from statstically obtained parses, some trees are ruled out before f-structure unification (Cahill et al., 2007), (ii) an Optimaly Theory-style constraint mechanism for filtering and ranking competing analyses (Frank et al., 2001), and (iii) a stochastic disambiguation component which is based on a log-linear probability model (Riezler et al., 2002) and works on the packed representations.

The German LFG grammar integrates a morphological component which is a variant of DMOR1 (Becker, 2001). This means that the (internal) lexicon does not comprise entries for surface word forms, but entries for specific morphological tags, see (Dipper, 2003).

3 Participles in the German LFG

3.1 Analysis

The morphosyntactic ambiguity of German participles presents a notorious difficulty for theoretical and computational analysis. The reason is that adjectives (i.e. adjectival participles) do not only occur as attributive modifiers (shown in (1-a)), but can also be used as predicatives (see (2-b)). These predicatives have exactly the same form as verbal or adverbial participles (compare the three sentences in (2)). Predicatives do appear either as arguments of verbs like *seem* or as free adjuncts such that they are not even syntactically distinguishable from adverbs. The sentence in (2-c) is thus ambiguous as to whether the participle is an adverb modifying the main verb, or a predicative which modifies the subject. Especially in the case of modifiers refering to a psychological state, the two underlying readings are hard to tell apart (Geuder, 2004). It is due to the lack of reliable semantic tests that the standard German tag set (Schiller et al., 1995) assigns the tag "ADJD" to predicative adjectives as well as adverbs.

(2) a. Das Experiment hat ihn **begeistert**.
'The experiment has enthused him.'
b. Er scheint von dem Experiment **begeistert**.
'He seems enthusiastic about the experiment.'
c. Er hat **begeistert** experimentiert.
'He has experimented in an enthusiastic way' or:
'He was enthusiastic when he experimented.'

For performance reasons, the German LFG does not cover free predicatives at the moment. In the context of our crosslingual induction approach, the distinction between predicatives and adverbs is rather straigtforward since we base our experiments on languages that have morphologically distinct forms for these categories. In the following, we will thus limit the discussion to adverbial participles and ignore the complexities related to predicative participles.

In the German LFG, the treatment of a given participle form is closely tight to the morphological analysis encoded in DMOR. In particular, adverbial participles can have different degrees of lexicalisation. For *bestimmt* (*probably*) in (3-a), which is completely lexicalised, the morphology proposes two analyses: (i) a participle tag of the verbal lemma *bestimmen* (*determine*) and (ii) an adverb tag for the lemma *bestimmt*. In this case, the LFG parsing algorithm will figure out which morphological analysis yields a syntactically well-formed analysis. For *gezielt* (*purposeful*) in (3-b), DMOR outputs, besides the participle analysis, an adjective tag for the lemma. However, the grammar can turn it into an adverb by a general adverb conversion rule for adjectives. The difficult case for the German LFG grammar is illustrated in (3-c) by means of the adverbial participle *wiederholt* (*repeatedly*). This participle is neither lexicalised as an adverb nor as an adjective, but it still can be used as an adverb.

(3) a. **Bestimmt** ist dieser Mann sehr traurig.
Probably is the man very sad.
b. Der Mann hat **gezielt** gehandelt.
The man has acted purposefully.
c. Der Mann hat **wiederholt** geweint.
The man has repeatedly cried.

To cover sentences like (3-c), the grammar needs to include a rule that allows adverb conversion for participles. Unfortunately, this rule is very costly in terms of the overall performance of the grammar, as is shown in the following section.

3.2 Assessing the Effect of Participle Ambiguity on the German LFG

In this section, we want to illustrate the effect of one specific grammar rule, i.e. the rule that generally allows for conversion of participles into adverbs. We perform a contrastive evaluation of two versions of the grammar: (i) the *No-Part-Adv* version which does not allow for adverb conversion (except for the lexicalised participles from DMOR), (ii) the *All-Part-Adv* version which allows every participle to be analysed as adverb. Otherwise, the two versions of the grammar are completely identical.

The comparison between the *All-Part-Adv* and *No-Part-Adv* grammar version pursues two major goals: On the one hand, we want to assess their overall quantitative performance on representative gold standard data, as it is common practice for statistical parsing systems. On the other hand, we are interested in getting a detailed picture of the quality of the grammar for parsing adverbial participles. These two goals do not necessarily go together since we know that the phenomenon is not very frequent in the data which we use for evaluation. Therefore, we do not only report accuracy on gold standard data in the following, but also focus on error analysis and describe ways of qualitatively assessing the grammar performance.

For evaluation, we use the TIGER treebank (Brants et al., 2002). We report grammar performance on the development set which consists of the first 5000 TIGER sentences, and statistical accuracy on the standard heldout set which comprises 371 sentences.

Quantitative Evaluation We first want to assess the quantitative impact of the phenomenon of adverbial participles in our evaluation data. We parse the heldout set storing all possible analyses obtained by both grammars, in order to compare the upperbound score that the both versions can optimally achieve (i.e. independently of the disambiguation quality). Then, we run the XLE evaluation in the "oracle" mode which means that the disambiguation compares all system analyses for a given sentence to its gold analysis, and chooses the best system analysis for computing accuracy. The upperbound f-score for both grammar versions is almost identical (at about 83.6%). This suggests that the phenomenon of adverbial participles does not occur in the heldout set.

If we run the grammar versions on a larger set of sentences, the difference in coverage becomes more obvious. In Table 1, we report the absolute number of parsed sentences, starred sentences (only receiving a partial or fragment parse), and the timeouts [1] on our standard TIGER development set. Not very surprisingly, the coverage of the *All-Part-Adv* version seems to be broader. However, this does not necessarily mean that the 40 additionally covered sentences all exhibit adverbial participles (see below). Moreover, Table 2 gives a first indication of the fact that the extended coverage comes at a price: the *All-Part-Adv* version massively increases the number of ambiguities per sentence. Related to this, in the *All-Part-Adv* version, the number of timeouts increases by 16% and parsing speed goes down by 6% compared to the *No-Part-Adv* version.

To assess the effect of the massively increased ambiguity rate and the bigger proportion of timeouts in *All-Part-Adv*, we perform a statistical evaluation of the two versions of the grammar against the heldout set, i.e. we compute f-score based

[1] Sentences whose parsing can not be finished in predefined amount of time, the maximally allowed parse time is set to 20 seconds.

Grammar	Parsed Sent.	Starred Sent.	Time-outs	Time in sec
No-Part-Adv	4301	608	90	6853
All-Part-Adv	4339	555	105	7265

Table 1: Coverage-based evaluation on the TIGER development set (sentences 1-5000), 4999 sentences total

Sent. length	Av. ambiguities per sent. *No-Part-Adv*	*All-Part-Adv*	Av. Incr.
1-10	2.95	3.3	11%
11-20	24.99	36.09	44%
21-30	250.4	343.76	37%
31-40	1929.06	2972.847	54%
41-50	173970.0	663310.4	429%

Table 2: Average number of ambiguities per sentence

on the parses that the XLE disambiguation selects as the most probable parse. Both versions use the same disambiguation model which results in a slightly biased comparison but still reflects the effect of increased ambiguity on the disambiguation component. In Table 3, we can see that the *All-Part-Adv* version performs significantly worse than the grammar version which does not capture adverbial participles. The spurious ambiguities and timeouts produced in *All-Part-Adv* have such a strong negative impact on the disambiguation component that it can not be outweighed by the extended coverage of the grammar.

Qualitative Evaluation The fact that the *All-Part-Adv* version generally increases parse ambiguity suggests that it produces a lot of undesired analyses for constructions not related to adverbial participles. To assess this assumption, we drew a random sample of 20 sentences out of the additionally covered 41 sentences and checked manually whether these contained an adverbial participle: Only 40% of these sentences are actually correctly analysed. In all other cases, the grammar lacks an analysis for a completely different phenomenon (mostly related to coordination), but obtains an (incorrect) analysis on the basis of the adverb conversion rule.

Grammar	Prec.	Rec.	F-Sc.	Time in sec
All-Part-Adv	83.80	76.71	80.1	666.55
No-Part-Adv	84.25	78.3	81.17	632.21

Table 3: Evaluation on the TIGER heldout set, 371 sentences total

As an example, Figure 1 presents two c-structure analyses for the sentence in (4) in the *All-Part-Adv* grammar. In the second c-structure (CS2), the participle *kritisiert* (*criticised*) is analysed as adverb modifing the main verb *haben* (*have*). This results in a very strange underlying f-structure, meaning something like *the Greens possess the SPD in a criticising manner*.

(4) Die Grünen haben die SPD kritisiert.
The Greens have the SPD criticised.
"The Greens have criticised the SPD"

3.3 Interim Conclusion

This section has illustrated an exemplary dilemma for parsing systems that aim broad-coverage and linguisitically motivated analyses at the same time. Since these systems need to explicitly address and represent ambiguities that purely statistical systems are able to conflate or ignore, their performance is not automatically improved by adding a specific rule for a specific phenomenon. Interestingly, the negative consequences affecting the quantitative (statistical) as well as the qualitative (linguistic) dimension of the grammar seem to be closely related: The overgenerating adverb conversion rule empirically leads to linguistically unmotivated analyses which causes problems for the disambiguation component. In the rest of the paper, we show how the adverbial analysis of participles can be reasonably constrained on the basis of a lexical resource induced from a parallel corpus.

4 Cross-Lingual Induction of Adverbial Participles

The intuition of the cross-lingual induction approach is that adverbial participles can be easily extracted from parallel corpora since in other languages (such as English or French) adverbs are often morphologically marked and easily labelled by statistical PoS taggers. As an example, consider the sentence in (5), extracted from Europarl, where the German participle *verstärkt* is translated by unambiguous adverbs in English and French (*increasingly* and *davantage*).

(5) a. Nach der Osterweiterung stehen die Zeichen **verstärkt** auf Liberalisierung.
b. Following enlargement towards the east, the emphasis is **increasingly** on liberalisation.

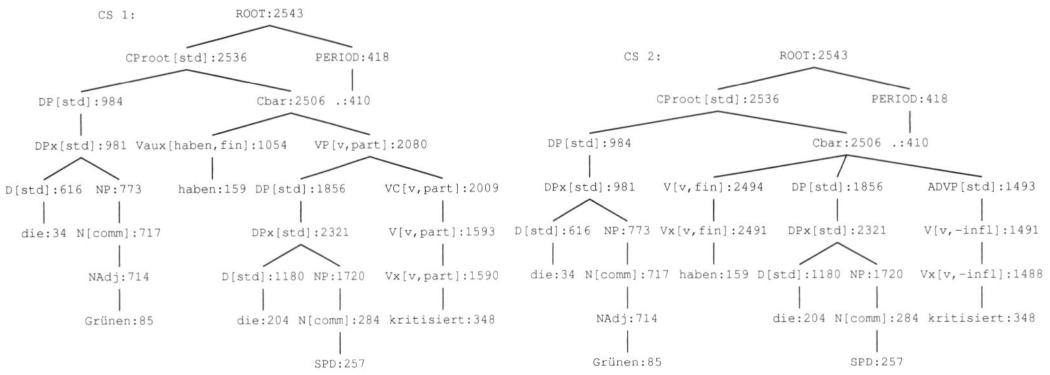

Figure 1: Two c-structures for sentence (4), obtained by the grammar *All-Part-Adv* - CS1 is correct, CS2 is semantically very strange

c. Après l' élargissement à l' Est, la tendance sera **davantage** à la libéralisation.

In the following, we describe experiments on Europarl where we automatically extract and filter adverbially translated German participles.

4.1 Data

We base our experiments on the German, English, French and Dutch part of the Europarl corpus. We automatically word-aligned the German part to each of the others with the GIZA++ tool (Och and Ney, 2003). Note that, due to divergences in sentence alignment and tokenisation, the three word-alignments are not completely synchronised. Moreover, each of the 4 languages has been automatically PoS tagged using the TreeTagger (Schmid, 1994). In addition, the German and English parts have been parsed with MaltParser (Nivre et al., 2006).

Since we want to limit our investigation to those participles that are not already recorded as lexicalised adjective or adverb in the DMOR morphology, we first have to generate the set of participle candidates from the tagged Europarl data. We extract all distinct words (types) from the German part that have been either tagged as ADJD (predicative or adverbial modifier), 6089 types in total, or as VVPP (past perfect participle), 5469 types in total. We intersect this set of potential participles with the set of DMOR participles that only have a verbal lemma. The resulting intersection (5054 types in total) constitutes the set of all German participles in Europarl that are not recorded as lexicalised in the DMOR morphology .

Given the participle candidates, we now extract the set of sentences that exhibit a word alignment between a German participle and an English, French or Dutch adverb. The extraction yields 5191 German-English sentence pairs, 2570 German-French, and 4129 German-Dutch sentence pairs. The German-English pairs comprise 1070 types of potentially adverbial participles. The types found in the German-French and German-Dutch part form a proper subset of the types extracted from the German-English pairs. Thus, the additional languages will not increase the recall of the induction. However, we will show that they are extremely useful for filtering incorrect or uninteresting participle alignments.

For data exploration and evaluation, we annotated 300 participle alignments out of the 5191 German-English sentences as to whether the English adverbial really points to an adverbial participle on the German side (and/or the word-alignment was correct). Throughout the entire set of annotated sentences, this ratio between the parallel cases (where an English adverbial correctly indicates a German adverbial) and all adverbially translated participles is at about 30%. This means that if we base the induction on word-alignments alone, its precision would be relatively low.

The remaining 60% translation pairs do not only reflect word alignment errors, but also cases where we find a proper participle in the German sentence that has a correct adverbial translation for other reasons. A typical configuration is exemplified in (6) where the German main verb *vorlegen* is translated as the verb-adverb combination *put forward*.

(6) a. Wir haben eine Reihe von Vorschlägen **vorgelegt**.
b. We have **put forward** a number of proposals.

These sentence pairs are cases of free or para-

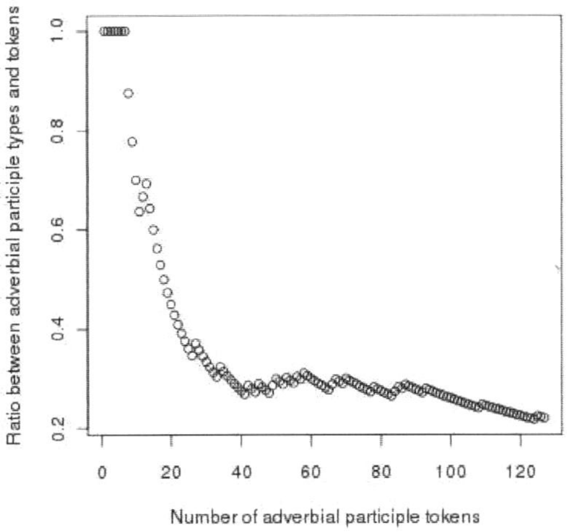

Figure 2: Type/token ratio for adverbial participles

phrasing translations. Ideally, we want our induction method to filter such type of configurations.

The 300 annotated sentences comprise 121 token instances of German adverbially used participles that have an adverbial translation in English. However, these 121 tokens reduce to 24 participle types. The graph in Figure 2 displays the type/token-ratio for an increasing number of instances in our gold standard. The curve exponentially decays from about 10 tokens onward and suggests that from about 30 tokens onward, the number of unseen types is relatively low. This can be interpreted as evidence in favour of the hypothesis that the number of adverbially used participles is actually fairly limited and can be integrated into the grammar in terms of a hard-coded resource.

4.2 Filtering

The data analysis in the previous section has shown that approximately one third of the English adverb alignments actually point to an adverbial participle on the German side. This means that we have to rigorously filter the data that we extract on the basis of word-alignments in order to obtain a high quality resource for our grammar. In this section, we will investigate several filtering methods and evaluate them on our annotated sentence pairs.

Frequency-based filtering As a first attempt, we filtered the non-parallel cases in our set of participle-adverb translations by means of the relative frequency of the adverb translations. For each participle candidate, we counted the number of tokens that exhibit an adverbial alignment on the English side, and divided this number by its total number of occurrences in the German Europarl. The best f-score of the ADV-FREQ filter (see Table 4) is achieved by the 0.05 threshold, but generally, the precision of the frequency filters is too low for high-quality resource induction. The reason for the poor performance of the frequency-based filters seems to be that some German verbs are systematically translated as verb - adverb combinations as in (6). For these participles, the relative frequency of adverbial alignments is not a good indicator for their adverbial use in German.

Multilingual Filtering Similar to filters used in annotation projection where noisy word-alignments are "cleaned" with the help of additional languages (Bouma et al., 2008), we have implemented a filter that only selects those participles as adverbials which also exhibit a certain amount of adverbial translations in the French and Dutch Europarl. We count the total number of adverbial translations of a given participle on the French side and divide it by the number of English adverbial translations. For French, the best f-score is achieved at a threshold of >0.1 (filter FR). For Dutch, the best f-score is achieved at a threshold of >0.05 (filter NL). The exact precision and recall values are given in Table 4.

Syntax-based Filtering The intuition behind the filters presented in this section is that adverbial translations which are due to cross-lingual divergences can be identified on the basis of their syntactic contexts. Information about these contexts can be extracted from the dependency analyses produced by MaltParser for the German and English data. On the German side, we want to exclude those participle instances for which the German parser has found an auxiliary head, since this configuration points to a normal partciple context in German. The filter is called G-HEAD in Table 4. It filters all types which have an auxiliary head in more than 40% of their adverbial translation configurations. On the English side, we exclude all translations where the adverb has a verbal head which is also aligned to the German partciple. The filter is called E-HEAD in Table 4. It excludes all participle types which exhibit the E-HEAD configuration in more than 50% of the cases.

filter	prec.	rec.	f-sc.
ADV-FREQ	0.38	0.75	0.51
FR	0.48	0.76	0.58
NL	0.33	0.73	0.45
G-HEAD	0.65	0.8	0.71
E-HEAD	0.4	0.8	0.53
COMBINED-1	0.61	0.8	0.69
COMBINED-2	0.86	0.76	0.81

Table 4: Performance of filters on the set of gold adverbial participle types

Combined Token-level Filtering So far, we have shown that multilingual and syntactic information is useful to filter non-parallel participle translations. We have found that the precision of the syntactic filters can still be increased by combining it with the multilingual filters. COMBINED-1 in Table 4 refers to the filter which only includes those participle types which have at least one adverbial translation on the English target side such that (i) the adverbial translation is paralleled on the French or Dutch target side for the same German participle token and (ii) the German participle token does not have an auxiliary head. If we combine this token-level filtering with the syntactic type-level filtering G-HEAD and E-HEAD (the filter called COMBINED-2 in Table 4), the precision increases by about 25% with little loss in recall.

4.3 Analysis

Based on the filtering techniques described in the previous section, we can finally induce a list of 46 German adverbial participles from Europarl. The fact that this participle class seems fairly delimited in our data raises the theoretical question whether the adverb conversion is licensed by any linguistic, i.e. lexical-semantic, properties of these participles. However, we observe that the automatically induced list comprises very diverse types of adverbs, as well as very distinct types of underlying verbs. Thus, besides adverbs that clearly modify events (see sentence (5)), we also found adverbs that are more likely to modify adjectives (sentence (7-a)), or propositions (sentence (7-b)).

(7) a. Es ist eine **verdammt** gefährliche Situation.
'It is a damned dangerous situation.'
b. Wir machen einen Bericht über den Bericht des Rechnungshofes , **zugegeben**.
'We are drafting a report about the report of the Court of Auditors , admittedly.'

A more fine-grained classification and analysis of adverbial participles is left for future research.

5 Grammar-based Evaluation

The resource of participles licensing adverbial use, whose induction was described in the previous section, can be straightforwardly integrated into the German LFG. By explicitly enumerating the participles in the adverb lexicon, the grammar can apply the standard adverb macros to them. To assess the effect of the filtering, we built two new versions of the grammar: (i) *Euro-Part-Adv*, its adverb lexicon comprises all adverbially translated participles found in Europarl (1091 types) and (ii) *Filt-Part-Adv*, its adverb lexicon comprises only the syntactically and multilingually filtered participles found in Europarl (46 types).

Although we have seen in section 3.2 that adverbial participles do not seem to occur in the TIGER heldout set, we also know that it is important to assess the effect of ambiguity rate on the overall grammar performance. Therefore, we computed the accuracy of the most probable parses produced by the *Euro-Part-Adv* and *Filt-Part-Adv* on the heldout set. As is shown in Table 5, the *Euro-Part-Adv* performs significantly worse than *Filt-Part-Adv*. This suggests that the non-filtered participle resource is not constrained enough and still produces a lot of spurious ambiguites that mislead the disambiguation component. The coverage values in Table 6 further corroborate the observation that the unfiltered participle resource behaves similar to the unrestricted adverb conversion in *All-Part-Adv* (see Section 3.2). The coverage of the filtered vs. the unfiltered version on the development set is identical, however the timeouts in *Euro-Part-Adv* increase by 17% and parsing time by 8%.

By contrast, there is no significant difference in f-score between the *No-Part-Adv* version presented in Section 3.2 and the *Filt-Part-Adv* version. Thus, we can, at least, assume that the filtered participles resources has restricted the massive overgeneration caused by the general adverb conversion rule such that the overall performance of the original grammar is not negatively affected.

To evaluate the participle resource as to whether it could have a positive qualtitative effect on parsing TIGER at all, we built a specialised testsuite which comprises only sentences containing a non-lexicalised participle, which has an adverbial translation in Europarl and is tagged as ADJD

Grammar	Prec.	Rec.	F-Sc.	Time in sec
Euro-Part-Adv	82.32	75.78	78.91	701
Filt-Part-Adv	84.12	78.2	81.05	665

Table 5: Evaluation on the TIGER heldout set, 371 sentences total

Grammar	Parsed Sent.	Starred Sent.	Time-outs	Time in sec
Euro-Part-Adv	4304	588	107	7359
Filt-Part-Adv	4304	604	91	6791

Table 6: Performance on the TIGER development set (sentences 1-5000), 4999 sentences total

in TIGER. The sentences were extracted from the whole TIGER corpus yielding a set of 139 sentences. In this quality-oriented evaluation, we only contrast the *No-Part-Adv* version with the filtered *Filt-Part-Adv* version since the unfiltered version leads to worse overall performance. As can be seen in Table 7, the *No-Part-Adv* can only completely cover 36% of the specialised testsuite which is much lower than its average complete coverage on the development set (86%). This suggests that a substantial number of the extracted ADJD participles are actually used as adverbial in the specialised testsuite.

Similar to the qualitative evaluation procedure in 3.2, we manually evaluated a random sample of 20 sentences covered by *Filt-Part-Adv* and not by *No-Part-Adv* as to whether they contain an adverbial participle that has been correctly recognised. This was the case for 90% of the sentences, the remaining 2 sentences were cases of secondary predications. An example of a relatively simple TIGER sentence that the grammar could not cover in the *No-Part-Adv* version is given in (8).

(8) Die Anti-Baby-Pillen stehen im Verdacht , **vermehrt** Thrombosen auszulösen.
"The birth control pill is suspected to **increasingly** cause thromboses."

We also manually checked a random sample of 20 sentences that the *Filt-Part-Adv* grammar could not cover, in order to see whether the grammar systematically misses certain cases of adverbial participles. In this second random sample, the percentage of sentences containing a true adverbial participle was again 90%. The grammar could not correctly analyse these because of their special syntax that is not covered by the general adverb macro (or, of course, because of difficult constructions not related to adverbial participles). An example for such a case is given in (9).

Grammar	Parsed Sent.	Starred Sent.	Time-outs	Time in sec
No-Part-Adv	50	77	12	427
Filt-Part-Adv	92	39	8	366

Table 7: Performance on the specialised TIGER test set, 139 sentences total

(9) Transitreisen junger Männer vom Gaza-Streifen ins Westjordanland und **umgekehrt** sind nicht gestattet.
"Transit travels from the Gaza Strip to the West Bank and **vice versa** are not allowed for young men."

The high proportion of true adverbial participle instances in our specific testsuite suggests that the data we induced from Europarl largely carries over to TIGER (despite genre differences, for instance) and constitutes a generally useful resource. Thus, we can not only say that the filtered participle resource has no negative effect on the overall performance of the German LFG, but also extends its coverage for a less frequent phenomenon in a linguistically precise way.

6 Conclusion

We have proposed an empirical account for detecting adverbial participles in German. Since this category is usually not annotated in German resources and hard to describe in theory, we based our method on multilingual parallel data. This data suggests that only a fairly limited class of participles actually undergo the conversion to adverbs in free text. We have described a set of linguistically motivated filters which are necessary to induce a high-precision resource for adverbial participles from parallel data. This resource has been integrated into the German LFG grammar. In contrast to the version of the grammar which does not restrict the participle - adverb conversion, the restricted version produces less spurious ambiguities which leads to better f-score on gold standard data. Moreover, by manually evaluating a specialised data set, we have established that the restricted version also extends the coverage and produces the correct analyses which can be used for further linguistic study.

References

Tanja Becker. 2001. DMOR: Handbuch. Technical report, IMS, University of Stuttgart.

Gerlof Bouma, Jonas Kuhn, Bettina Schrader, and Kathrin Spreyer. 2008. Parallel LFG Grammars on Parallel Corpora: A Base for Practical Triangulation. In Miriam Butt and Tracy Holloway King, editors, *Proceedings of the LFG08 Conference*, pages 169–189, Sydney, Australia. CSLI Publications, Stanford.

Sabine Brants, Stefanie Dipper, Silvia Hansen, Wolfgang Lezius, and George Smith. 2002. The tiger treebank. In *Proceedings of the Workshop on Treebanks and Linguistic Theories*.

Joan Bresnan. 2000. *Lexical-Functional Syntax*. Blackwell, Oxford.

Miriam Butt, Helge Dyvik, Tracy Holloway King, Hiroshi Masuichi, and Christian Rohrer. 2002. The Parallel Grammar Project.

Aoife Cahill, John T. Maxwell III, Paul Meurer, Christian Rohrer, and Victoria Rosén. 2007. Speeding up LFG Parsing using C-Structure Pruning . In *Coling 2008: Proceedings of the workshop on Grammar Engineering Across Frameworks*, pages 33 – 40.

Stefanie Dipper. 2003. *Implementing and Documenting Large-Scale Grammars — German LFG*. Ph.D. thesis, Universität Stuttgart, IMS.

Anette Frank, Tracy Holloway King, Jonas Kuhn, and John T. Maxwell. 2001. Optimality Theory Style Constraint Ranking in Large-Scale LFG Grammars . In Peter Sells, editor, *Formal and Empirical Issues in Optimality Theoretic Syntax*, page 367–397. CSLI Publications.

Wilhelm Geuder. 2004. Depictives and transparent adverbs. In J. R. Austin, S. Engelbrecht, and G. Rauh, editors, *Adverbials. The Interplay of Meaning, Context, and Syntactic Structure*, pages 131–166. Benjamins.

Philipp Koehn. 2005. Europarl: A parallel corpus for statistical machine translation. In *MT Summit 2005*.

Joakim Nivre, Johan Hall, and Jens Nilsson. 2006. Maltparser: A data driven parser-generator for dependency parsing. In *Proc. of LREC-2006*.

Franz Josef Och and Hermann Ney. 2003. A systematic comparison of various statistical alignment models. *Computational Linguistics*, 29(1):19–51.

Stefan Riezler, Tracy Holloway King, Ronald M. Kaplan, Richard Crouch, John T. Maxwell, and Mark Johnson. 2002. Parsing the Wall Street Journal using a Lexical-Functional Grammar and Discriminative Estimation Techniques . In *Proceedings of ACL 2002*.

Christian Rohrer and Martin Forst. 2006. Improving coverage and parsing quality of a large-scale LFG for German. In *Proceedings of LREC-2006*.

Anne Schiller, Simone Teufel, and Christine Thielen. 1995. Guidelines fuer das Tagging deutscher Textkorpora mit STTS. Technical report, IMS, University of Stuttgart.

Helmut Schmid. 1994. Probabilistic part-of-speech tagging using decision trees. In *Proceedings of International Conference on New Methods in Language Processing*.

David Yarowsky, Grace Ngai, and Richard Wicentowski. 2001. Inducing multilingual text analysis tools via robust projection across aligned corpora. In *Proceedings of HLT 2001, First International Conference on Human Language Technology Research*.

You talking to me? A predictive model for zero auxiliary constructions

Andrew Caines
Computation, Cognition & Language Group
RCEAL, University of Cambridge, UK
apc38@cam.ac.uk

Paula Buttery
Computation, Cognition & Language Group
RCEAL, University of Cambridge, UK
pjb48@cam.ac.uk

Abstract

As a consequence of the established practice to prefer training data obtained from written sources, NLP tools encounter problems in handling data from the spoken domain. However, accurate models of spoken data are increasingly in demand for naturalistic speech generation and machine translations in speech-like contexts (such as chat windows and SMS). There is a widely held assumption in the linguistic field that spoken language is an impoverished form of written language. However, we show that spoken data is not unpredictably irregular and that language models can benefit from detailed consideration of spoken language features. This paper considers one specific construction which is largely restricted to the spoken domain - the ZERO AUXILIARY - and makes a predictive model of that construction for native speakers of British English. The model can predict zero auxiliary occurrence in the BNC with 96.9% accuracy. We will demonstrate how this model can be integrated into existing parsing tools, increasing the number of successful parses for this zero auxiliary construction by around 30%, and thus improving the performance of NLP applications which rely on parsing.

1 Introduction

Up to this point, statistical Natural Language Processing (NLP) tools have generally been trained on corpora that are representative of written rather than spoken language. A major factor behind this decision to use written data is that it is far easier to collect than spoken data. Newswire, for instance, may be harvested readily and in abundance. Once collected, written language requires relatively little processing before it can be used for training a statistical model.

Processing of spoken data, on the other hand, involves at the very least transcription - which usually requires a human transcriber. Since transcription is a slow and laborious task, the collection of spoken data is highly resource intensive. But this relative difficulty in collection is not the only reason that spoken language data has been sidelined. Had spoken data been considered to be crucial to the production of NLP applications greater efforts might have been made to obtain it. However, on account of some of its characteristic features such as hesitations, interruptions and ellipsis, spoken language is often dismissed as nothing more than a noisy approximation to 'real' or 'intended' language.

In some forums, written language is held up as an idealised form of language toward which speakers aspire and onto which spoken language should be retrofitted. This is an artefact of the theoretical notion of a 'competence'-'performance' dichotomy (Chomsky 1965) with the latter deemed irrelevant and ignored in mainstream linguistic research.

The consequence of the established practice to sideline spoken data is that NLP tools are inherently error prone when handling data from the spoken domain. With increasing calls for speech to be considered the primary form of language and to be treated as such (Sampson 2001: 7 [1]; Cermák 2009: 115 [2]; Haugh 2009: 74 [3]) and a growing trend for NLP techniques to be integrated into cognitive and neurolinguistic research as well as forensic appli-

[1]Speech is "unquestionably the more natural, basic mode of language behaviour".

[2]"From a linguistic point of view, spoken corpora should be primary for research but that has not been the case so far".

[3]Haugh observes that "spoken language and interaction lie at the core of human experience" but bemoans the "relative neglect of spoken language in corpora to date".

Proceedings of the 2010 Workshop on NLP and Linguistics: Finding the Common Ground, ACL 2010, pages 43–51,
Uppsala, Sweden, 16 July 2010.

cations, there are now compelling reasons to examine spoken data more closely. Accurate models of spoken data are increasingly in demand for naturalistic speech generation and machine translations in speech-like contexts (such as human-machine dialogue, chat windows and SMS).

The main research aim of our work is to show that spoken data should not be considered error prone and therefore unpredictably irregular. We show that language models can be improved in increments as we deepen our understanding of spoken language features. We investigate ZERO AUXILIARY progressive aspect constructions - those which do not feature the supposedly obligatory auxiliary verb, as in (1a) below (cf. 1b):

(1a) What you doing? Who you looking for? You been working?

(1b) What are you doing? Who are you looking for? Have you been working?

The zero auxiliary is a non-standard feature which for the most part is known to be restricted to speech. A corpus study of spoken British English indicates that in progressive aspect interrogatives with second person subjects (as in (1) above) the auxiliary occurs in zero form in 27% of constructions found. The equivalent figure from the written section of the corpus is just 5.4%. Consequently, existing NLP techniques - since they are based on written training data - are unlikely to deal appropriately with zero auxiliary constructions. We report below on the corpus study in full and use the results of logistic regression to design a predictive model of zero auxiliary occurrence in spoken English. The model is based on contextual grammatical features and can predict zero auxiliary occurrence in the British National Corpus (BNC; 2007) with 96.9% accuracy. Finally, we discuss how this model can be used to improve the performance of NLP techniques in the spoken domain, demonstrating its implementation in the RASP system (Robust Accurate Statistical Parsing; (Briscoe, Carroll and Watson, 2006)).

This paper underlines why awareness of non-standard linguistic features matters. Targeted data extraction from large corpus resources allows the construction of more informed language models which have been trained on naturalistic spoken usage rather than standard and restricted rules of written language. Such work has only been made possible with the advent of large spoken language corpora such as the BNC. Even so, the resource-heavy nature of spoken data collection means that speech transcriptions constitute only one tenth of this 100 million word corpus [4]. Nevertheless, it is an invaluable resource made up of a range of speech genres including spontaneous face-to-face conversation, a fact which makes it unique among corpora. Since conversational dialogue is the predominant language medium, the BNC offers the best chance of modelling speech as it occurs naturally.

This work has important implications for both computational and theoretical linguistics. On the one hand, we can improve various NLP techniques with more informed language models, and on the other hand we are reminded that the space of grammatical possibility is not restricted and that continued empirical investigation is key in order to arrive at the fullest possible description of language use.

2 Spoken and written language

In the modern mainstream fields of linguistic research, based on Chomsky's 'ideal speaker-listener' (1965), spoken language has been all too easily dismissed from consideration on the grounds that it is more error-prone and less important than written language. In this idealisation, the speaker-listener is "unaffected by such grammatically irrelevant conditions as memory limitations, distractions, shifts of attention and interest, and errors (random or characteristic)" (Chomsky, 1965).

The 'errors' Chomsky refers to are features of speech production such as pauses, filled silence, hesitation, repetition and elision, or of dialogue such as backgrounding, overlap and truncation between speakers. Thus 'error' is essentially here defined as that which is not normally found in well-formed written data, that which is 'noisy' and 'unpredictable'. It is on these grounds - the grammatical rigidity of the written medium relative to speech - that the divide between spoken and written language modelling has grown up.

The opposing, usage-based view is that spoken language is systematic and that it should be modelled as it is rather than as a crude approximation of the written form. On this view, the speech production and dialogue features listed above are not

[4]Cermák estimates our experience with each language medium is in fact this ratio in reverse - 90:10 spoken to written (2009: 115).

considered mistakes but "regular products of the system of spoken English" (Halliday, 1994). 'Error' is thus seen as a misnomer for these features because they are in fact all regular in some way. For example, the fact that people tend to put filler pauses in specific places.

We propose a middle way: that which builds on the NLP tools available, even though they are trained on written data, and on top of these models the features of spoken language as 'noise' in the communicative channel. This is a pragmatic approach which recognises the considerable amount of work underpinning existing NLP tools and sees no value in discarding these and starting again from scratch. We demonstrate that spoken language is model-able and predictable, even with a feature which would not be seen as 'correct' in written form. For practical purposes we need to recognise the regularities in the apparently 'incorrect' features of speech and build these into the functioning language models we already have through statistical analysis of corpus distributions and appropriate adjustment to parser tools.

3 The zero auxiliary construction

According to standard grammatical rules, the auxiliary verb is an obligatory feature of progressive aspect constructions. However, this rule is based on norms of written language and is in fact not always adhered to in the production of speech. As a result, some progressive constructions do not feature an auxiliary verb. These are termed 'zero auxiliary' constructions and have been previously examined in studies of dialect (Labov, 1969; Andersen, 1995) and first language acquisition (Brown, 1973; Rizzi, 1993/1994; Wexler, 1994; Lieven et al, 2003; Wilson, 2003; Theakston et al, 2005).

There are copious anecdotal examples of the zero auxiliary:

(2) You talking to me? Travis Bickle in *Taxi Driver* (1976).

(3) Where he going? Avon Barksdale in *The Wire*, Season 1: 'Game Day' (2002).

(4) What you doing? Holly Golightly in *Breakfast at Tiffany's* (1961).

Natural language data taken from the spoken section of the British National Corpus (sBNC) shows that the zero auxiliary features in 1330 (27%) of the 4923 second person progressive interrogative constructions; as in (1), (2), (4) above. In first person singular declaratives (cf. (5a) and (5b)), in contrast, the proportion of zero auxiliary occurrence is just 0.9% (158 of 17,838 constructions). This already indicates the way that the zero auxiliary occurs in predictable contexts and how grammatical properties will feature in the predictive model.

(5a) What I saying? I annoying you? Why I doing this?

(5b) What am I saying? Am I annoying you? Why am I doing this?

Subject person, subject number, subject type (pronoun or other noun) and clause type (declarative or interrogative) are four of the eight syntactic properties incorporated in the predictive model. The four other properties are clause tense (6), perfect or non-perfect aspect (7), clause polarity (8) and presence or absence of subject (9).

(6) You are debugging. You were debugging.

(7) We have been looking for a present. We are looking for a present.

(8) She is watching the grand prix. He is not watching the grand prix.

(9) I am going to town in a minute. Going to town in a minute.

We employ logistic regression to investigate the precise nature of the relationships between zero auxiliary use and these various linguistic variables. This allows us to build a predictive model of zero auxiliary occurrence in spoken language which will be useful for several reasons relating to parsing of natural spoken language. Firstly, for automatic parsing of spoken data being able to predict when a zero auxiliary is likely to occur enables the parser to relax its normal rules which are based on written standards. Secondly, as technology improves and interaction with computers becomes more humanistic the need to replicate human-like communication increases in importance: by knowing in which contexts the auxiliary verb might be absent, researchers can build a language model which is more realistic and so the user experience is improved and made more naturalistic. Thirdly, a missing auxiliary might be problematic for machine translation since it could result in the loss of tense and aspect information, but with the ability to predict where a zero auxiliary might occur, the auxiliary can be restored so that translation can be performed with appropriate tense and aspect.

For all these reasons, the zero auxiliary in spoken English is an appropriate case study for finding the common ground between NLP and Linguistics. Awareness of this particular linguistic phenomenon through corpus study allows the construction of more informed language models which in turn enhance relevant NLP techniques. The cross-pollination of research from NLP and linguistics benefits both fields and ties in with the emergence of linguistic theories that "conceive of structure as gradient, malleable and probabilistic" and incorporate "knowledge of the frequency and probability of use of these categories in speakers' experience" (Tily et al, 2009). These are collectively known as 'usage-based' approaches to language theory and are exerting a growing influence on the field (e.g. Barlow and Kemmer 2000; Bybee and Hopper 2001; Bod, Hay and Jannedy 2003).

4 Corpus study

Training data was obtained through manual annotation of progressive constructions in the British National Corpus (2007). A preliminary study of interrogatives with second person subjects confirmed that the zero auxiliary is more a feature of the spoken rather than the written domain (Table 1). Therefore a focus on the spoken section of the corpus (sBNC) was justified and so we undertook a comprehensive study of all progressive constructions in sBNC. The genres contained in sBNC include a range of settings and levels of formality - from academic lectures to radio programmes to spontaneous, face-to-face conversation.

We extracted 93,253 sentences featuring a progressive construction from sBNC and each was manually annotated for auxiliary realisation and the eight syntactic properties described in Table 2. In Table 3 the progressive constructions are classified by auxiliary realisation. With approximately 4.2% occurrence in progressive constructions, zero auxiliaries are a low frequency feature of spoken language but ones which are significant for the fact that existing NLP tools cannot successfully parse them, thus one in twenty-five progressive constructions will not be fully parsed. We use the annotated corpus of these progressive constructions to design the predictive model described below.

Corpus	**Auxiliary**		
	Full	**Contracted**	**Zero**
wBNC	3220	27	187
sBNC	3498	95	1330

Table 1: Auxiliary realisation in second person progressive interrogatives in the BNC.

Properties	Value encodings
Aux realisation	
Zero auxiliary	full(0), contracted(1), zero(2)
Variables	
Subject person	1st(1), 2nd(2), 3rd(3)
Subject number	singular(0), plural(1)
Subject type	other noun(0), pronoun(1)
Subj supplied	zero subj(0), subj supplied(1)
Clause type	declarative(0), interrogative(1)
Clause tense	present(0), past(1)
Perfect aspect	non-perfect(0), perfect(1)
Polarity	positive(0), negative(1)

Table 2: Syntactic features and their encodings in the annotated sBNC Progressive Corpus

5 Model

To predict the zero auxiliary in spoken language we use logistic regression. To train this model we took a 90% sample from our corpus of 93,253 progressive constructions extracted from the spoken section of the BNC, as described above and in Caines 2010. The dataset was split into two categories: those sentences which exhibited the zero auxiliary and those which did not[5]. A logistic regression was then performed to ascertain the probability of category membership using the eight previously described syntactic properties. Note that subject person is arguably not a scalar vari-

[5]Contracted auxiliaries thus belong in the 'not zero auxiliary' category.

Corpus	**Full**	**Contracted**	**Zero**
sBNC	38,015	51,295	3943

Table 3: Auxiliary realisation in progressive constructions in sBNC.

able and therefore is re-analysed as three boolean variables with separate binary values for use of the first, second and third person. However, the three subject person variables are dependent (*ie.* If the subject is not first or second person it will be in the third). Thus the eight syntactic properties become nine explanatory variables in the predictive model, as reported in Table 4.

Corpus	Predictor Coefficient
subject person: 1st	0.171
subject person: 2nd	1.280
plural subject	-0.300
pronoun subject	-0.470
zero subject	5.711
interrogative clause	2.139
past tense clause	-4.852
perfect aspect	-0.280
negated clause	-1.163
constant	-4.033

Table 4: Predictor coefficients for the presence of a zero auxiliary construction.

5.1 Model Evaluation

The logistic function is defined by:

$$f(Z) = \frac{1}{1+e^{-z}} \quad (1)$$

The variable z is representative of the set of predictors and is defined by:

$$z = \beta_0 + \beta_1 x_1 + \beta_2 x_2 + \ldots + \beta_k x_k \quad (2)$$

where β_0, β_1, β_2 ... β_k are the regression coefficients of predictors x_1, x_2 .. x_k respectively. The predictors explored in this paper are encodings of the syntactic properties of the annotated sentences. The predictors and their encodings are indicated in Table 2.

The logistic function is constrained to values between 0 and 1 and represents the probability of membership of one of the two categories (zero auxiliary or auxiliary supplied). In our case an $f(z) > 0.5$ indicates that there is likely to be a zero auxiliary.

The logistic function defined by the coefficients in Table 4 is able to predict correct category membership for 96.9% of the sentences in the annotated corpus. All coefficients are highly significant to the logistic function ($p<0.001$) with the exception of perfect aspect and first person subject - which are both significant nevertheless ($p<0.05$).

For this model, positive coefficients indicate that the associated syntactic properties raise the probability of a zero auxiliary occurring. Large coefficients more strongly influence the probability of the zero auxiliary whereas near-zero coefficients have little influence. From the coefficients in Table 4 we see that the strongest predictor of a zero auxiliary is the occurrence of a zero subject (as in the utterance, *'leaving now.'*). An interrogative utterance is also a good candidate, as is the second person subject (e.g. *'you eating those olives?'*). However, a past tense utterance is an unlikely candidate for a zero auxiliary construction, as is a negated utterance.

6 Discussion — using the predictive model to aid parsing

As mentioned above, since parsers are trained on written data they can often display poor performance on text transcribed from the spoken domain. From the results of our corpus study we know that the zero auxiliary occurs in approximately 4.2% of progressive constructions in spoken language and we can extrapolate that it will occur in less than 1% (approximately 0.8%) of all progressive constructions in written language. A statistical parser trained on written language will therefore be prone to undergo parsing failure for every one in twenty-five progressive sentences. This is no insignificant problem, especially when it is remarked that the progressive is in high frequency usage (there are one thousand ING-forms featuring in progressive constructions for every one million words of sBNC) and that its use is known to be spreading (Leech et al, 2009).

Compounded with those parser breakdowns caused by other speech phenomena (for instance, repetition and elision), high numbers of parse failures on progressive constructions will render NLP accuracy on spoken language intolerable for any applications which rely on accurate parsing as a foundation. However, we have shown above that features of spoken language such as the zero auxiliary should not be thought of as errors or as unpredictable deviations from the written form, but rather can be considered to be consistent and predictable events. In this section we illustrate how our predictive model for zero auxiliary occurrence

$$(|relation|\ |head|\ |dependant|) \quad (3)$$
$$(|ncsubj|\ |play+ing:VVG|\ |you:PPY|) \quad (4)$$
$$(|obj|\ |play+ing:VVG|\ |what:DDQ|) \quad (5)$$
$$(|aux|\ |play+ing:VVG|\ |be+:VBR|) \quad (6)$$
$$(|arg|\ |play+ing:VVG|\ |you:PPY|) \quad (7)$$
$$(|relation|\ |verb:VVG|\ |dependant|) \quad (8)$$

Figure 1: Example grammatical relations from RASP.

may be integrated into a parser pipeline in order to aid the parsing of spoken language. In this way we build on the increasingly robust engineering of statistical NLP tools trained on written language by allowing them to adapt to the spoken domain on the basis of the linguistic study of speech phenomena.

In general the notion of 'parsing' an utterance involves a chain of several processes: utterance boundary detection, tokenization, part-of-speech tagging, and then parsing. We suggest that when it is known that the language to be parsed is from the spoken domain the pipeline of processes should be run in a SPEECH AWARE MODE. Extra functionality would be incorporated into each of the stages according to the findings of linguistic research into spoken language. In other work we have adapted the tokenization and tagging stages of the pipeline based on predictors that indicate when interjections (e.g. *'umm'*, *'err'* and *'ah'*) have been 'used' as punctuation or lexical items. We also incorporate intonation phrases as predictors for utterance boundary detection (Buttery and Caines: in preparation). Here, we augment the parsing stage of the pipeline by allowing an informed re-parse of utterances in which a parse failure is likely to have been caused by a zero auxiliary.

We present this section with reference to the specific mechanics and output formats of the RASP system but our algorithm is by no means parser specific and could be adapted for other parsers quite easily. Utterances parsed with RASP may be expressed as 'grammatical relations'. RASP's grammatical relations are theory-general, binary relations between lexical terms and are expressed in the form of head-dependancy relations as shown in (3), Figure 1.

Consider the utterance *'what are you playing?'*. When we parse this with RASP we get grammatical relations (4), (5) and (6) in Figure 1. The capital letter codes following the ':' symbols are part-of-speech tags (from the CLAWS-2 tagset (Garside, 1987)) which have been assigned to the lexical tokens by the tagger of the RASP system. Here *PPY* indicates the pronoun *'you'*; *VVG* indicates the ING-form of lexical verb; *VBR* indicates *'be'* in 3rd person present tense; and *DDQ* indicates a wh-determiner. The relation (4) tells us that *'you'* is the subject of *'playing'*; relation (5) tells us that *'what'* is taking the place of the object being played; and relation (6) tells us that there is an auxiliary relationship between *'are'* and *'playing'*. This is much as we would expect. However, if we try to parse *'what you playing?'* the parse fails. The single relation (4) is returned where ideally we would like both (4) and (5), as we did when the auxiliary was present.

For the utterance, *'you playing?'* RASP returns the under-specified grammatical relation (7) which is simply indicating that *'you'* is an argument of *'playing'* but not which type of argument (whether a subject, direct object, etc). Ideally we would like to retrieve at least (4) as we would have if we parsed the utterance *'are you playing?'*. For these examples, we shall consider the failure to identify the correct subject and object of the progressive verb to be a parsing failure.

We integrate the zero auxiliary predictive model with parsing technology to improve the parsing of zero auxiliaries in spoken language. Note that we use the RASP system but our algorithm is by no means parser specific. The only prerequisite is that the parser must be able to identify relations of some kind between the subject noun and ING-form (possibly via a parsing rule) and also be able extract values for the predictors (through either a rich tagset or from the identification of key speech tokens). The illustrative method we discuss here is integrated into the parsing pipeline in the event of a parse failure but there are several alternative methods that might also be considered.

For instance, by using the predictive model earlier in the parsing system pipeline a modified tagset could be used which updates the ING-form tag with a new tag to indicate that there is also a missing auxiliary. Another method might involve altering rule probabilities or adding extra parser rules so that parsing only has to occur once. Our other work in this area suggests that the final decision on where to add the spoken language modifications within the parsing pipeline will largely depend on the interaction of the phenomena in question with other speech phenomena.[6]

With the proviso that it is a preliminary integration of the predictive model into a parsing system, we propose the following algorithm for zero auxiliaries in spoken language. When 'speech aware mode' is activated, if we encounter a parse failure then we first check the part-of-speech tags of the utterance to ascertain if the sentence contains the ING-form requisite for a progressive construction:

- **IF no ING-form is found**: STOP. Our model predicts zero auxiliaries in progressive constructions—there is nothing more we can do with the input.
- **ELSE**: An ING-form is found. Extract all grammatical relations that were obtained by the parse which contained the ING-form in the head position (these would be grammatical relations that have the general format of (8) in Figure 1). We will refer to this set of grammatical relations as GRS.
  - **IF there is an auxiliary relation present in** GRS: STOP. If at least one of the extracted grammatical relations is an auxiliary relation, similar to (6) in Figure 1, an auxiliary is present—we do not have a zero auxiliary construction.[7]
  - **ELSE**: The utterance is a candidate for zero auxiliary.

Having determined a possible candidate for zero auxiliary we carry out the following steps:

1. Ascertain values for the zero auxiliary predictors (explained in more detail below).
2. Calculate the value of the logistic function $f(z)$ using the obtained predictor values with their coefficients (shown in Table 4).
3. If $f(z) > 0.5$, assume an auxiliary is missing.
4. Add the auxiliary to the sentence (choosing which auxiliary based on the predictor values—see below).
5. Re-parse the sentence.
6. Remove (or flag) the auxiliary grammatical relation from the newly obtained parser output.[8]

For step 1 above properties of the current utterance have to be obtained. The subject person, plural subject, zero subject and pronoun subject properties are ascertained by looking at the part-of-speech of the dependant noun/pronoun within any subject relations occurring in the set GRS (grammatical relations headed by the ING-form). Subject relations would look similar to (4) in Figure 1. If there is no subject grammatical relation, any underspecified 'arg' relation (such as (7) in Figure 1) are considered. If neither of these relations are present in GRS then a zero subject is inferred. The person and plurality of the subject noun is encoded within its CLAWS2 part-of-speech tag. For instance, a *PPHS1* tag, which is used to indicate *'him'* or *'her'* would tell us we have a third person, singular pronoun.[9]

The other properties are all ascertained by the presence or absence of a token within the utterance: interrogative property is inferred when the utterance ends with a question mark; the negation property when either *'not'* or *'n't'* (which are tagged *XX*) is present; the perfect is inferred from the presence of the word *'been'*; and past tense is ascertained from a set of temporal marker lexical items (e.g. *'yesterday*, *'before'*). Once extracted the properties are encoded as shown in Table 4 for use as the predictor values in the logistic function.

In order to select the correct auxiliary and location for insertion in step 4 the utterance values are consulted. For instance, an interrogative utterance in the present tense, not in perfect aspect, with a second person singular subject will require insertion of the auxiliary *'are'* after the subject. A zero subject zero auxiliary, on the other hand, requires restoration of both subject and auxiliary. Where a question mark indicates it has been used in an interrogative clause the subject is assumed to be sec-

[6]Although, another major consideration is the overall computational efficiency of the parsing system.

[7]This step is actually subtly more complicated—auxiliary relations involving *'been'* are allowed to be present in GRS (this allows us to capture zero auxiliaries in the perfect such as *'been coming here long?'*) but if there is any other auxiliary relation present in GRS then we STOP here.

[8]We also remove (or flag) the subject relation in cases where a subject also had to be added in step 4. This would occur when the original utterance exhibited a zero subject.

[9]All common nouns are assumed to be 3rd person and all instances of *'you'* were considered to be singular (as was the case during corpus annotation).

ond person - as is the case in most questions - and so the auxiliary-subject combination *'are you'* is restored before the ING-form. Without a question mark, the clause is assumed to be declarative and so the first person singular subject-auxiliary combination *'I am'* is restored before the ING-form [10].

We withheld 10% of the zero auxiliary corpus for test purposes. The integration of the predictive model into the parser allowed us to successfully parse 31.4% of previously unparsable zero-auxilaries. On cleaned spoken transcripts (i.e. with speech phenomena other than the zero auxiliary, such as repetitions, removed) this algorithm allows us to retrieve the correct subject-object relations for an extra 1238 utterances within our annotated corpus (which again accounts for approximately one third of the previously unparsable zero-auxilaries). This is a significant step forward for any applications building on top of a parsing infrastructure.

7 Conclusion

We have shown how awareness of a specific linguistic phenomenon enables improvements in NLP techniques. The zero auxiliary is mainly a feature of spoken language and so is not on the whole handled successfully by existing parsers, trained as they are on written data. As a solution, rather than proposing the construction of new models specifically designed for spoken language, thereby doing away with all previous work on NLP tools and starting again from scratch, we demonstrated how new training data from a spoken source could be applied to an existing parser - RASP. We designed a predictive model of zero auxiliary occurrence based on logistic regression with nine syntactic variables. The data came from an annotated corpus of 93,253 progressive constructions which showed zero auxiliary frequency to be 4.2%. Without this new predictive information in the parser, the status quo would continue whereby one in twenty-five progressive constructions would continue to be mis-parsed. We found that instead the noise was regular and could be modelled, and we illustrated how this specific linguistic data could be integrated into existing NLP technology. This is a case study of one specific linguistic phenomenon. Our belief is that other such spoken language phenomena can be modelled in the same way, given an appropriate corpus resource, accurate annotation and implementation into a parser.

By running in a 'speech aware mode' which supplements existing parsing architecture we benefit from the training that has already been undertaken on a large scale based on written data and complement it with specialized and predictable linguistic properties of speech. Ideally, we would like to train an entire parsing system on spoken language but until spoken corpora become more readily available this is not a practical option: the resulting parser would suffer greatly from data sparsity issues. Frustratingly, there is a circular problem in generating corpora of an appropriate size for training since until highly accurate models for spoken language are built we can not expect speech-to-text systems to provide highly accurate transcripts. But to build these highly accurate models of spoken language in the first place a large amount of data is required. Augmenting the existing statistical NLP tools trained on written language with specialized linguistic knowledge from the spoken domain is a pragmatic short-term fix for this problem.

We should note that tailoring parsers to deal with spoken language is by no means unheard of: the RASP system itself, for example (which parses using a probabilistic context-free grammar), already has several rules in its grammar which are more appropriate for parsing spoken language. However, use of these rules can contribute to much over-generation and complexity in the parse forest (the parser internal structure which holds all the possible parses for an utterance). In consequence, the specialized rules have to be expertly selected or deselected when configuring the parser. This work - and our research program as a whole - would instead allow parser configuration decisions and algorithmic adaptions to be made non-expertly and on-the-fly when running in 'speech aware mode'. All rule activations and algorithm adaptions would be made based on predictions constructed from expert linguistic analysis of the spoken domain.

Acknowledgements

This work was supported by the AHRC. We thank three anonymous reviewers for their comments, Andrew Rice and Barbara Jones.

[10] A sample of one hundred zero subject declarative zero auxiliaries indicates that the first person singular is the appropriate subject type to restore on 60% of occasions.

References

Gisle Andersen. 1995. Omission of the primary verbs BE and HAVE in London teenage speech - a sociolinguistic study. Hovedfag thesis, University of Bergen, Norway.

Michael Barlow and Suzanne Kemmer. 2000. *Usage-based models of language*. Chicago: CSLI.

Rens Bod, Jennifer Hay and Stefanie Jannedy (eds.). 2003. *Probabilistic Linguistics*. Cambridge, MA: MIT Press.

Ted Briscoe, John Carroll and Rebecca Watson. 2007. The second release of the RASP system. *Proceedings of the COLING/ACL on Interactive presentation sessions*, July 17-18, 2006, Sydney, Australia.

The British National Corpus, version 3. 2007. Distributed by Oxford University Computing Services on behalf of the BNC Consortium. URL: http://www.natcorp.ox.ac.uk/

Roger Brown. 1973. *A First Language: the early stages*. London: George Allen and Unwin.

Paula Buttery and Andrew Caines. In preparation. *An Empirical Approach to First Language Acquisition*. Cambridge: Cambridge University Press.

Joan Bybee and Paul Hopper (eds.). 2001. *Frequency and the emergence of linguistic structure*. Amsterdam: John Benjamins.

Andrew Caines. 2010. *You talking to me?* Zero auxiliary constructions in British English. Ph.D thesis, University of Cambridge.

Frantisek Cermák. 2009. Spoken corpora design. Their constitutive parameters. *International Journal of Corpus Linguistics* 14: 113-123.

Noam Chomsky. 1965. *Aspects of the Theory of Syntax*. Cambridge, MA: MIT Press.

Roger Garside. 1987. The CLAWS Word-tagging System. In: Roger Garside, Geoffrey Leech and Geoffrey Sampson (eds.), *The Computational Analysis of English: A Corpus-based Approach*. London: Longman.

Michael A. K. Halliday. 1994. Spoken and Written Modes of Meaning. In: David Graddol and Oliver Boyd-Barrett (eds.), *Media Texts: Authors and Readers*. Clevedon: Multilingual Matters.

Michael Haugh. 2009. Designing a Multimodal Spoken Component of the Australian National Corpus. In: Michael Haugh, Kate Burridge, Jean Mulder, and Pam Peters (eds.), *Selected Proceedings of the 2008 HCSNet Workshop on Designing the Australian National Corpus*. Somerville, MA: Cascadilla Proceedings Project.

William Labov. 1969. Contraction, deletion, and inherent variability of the English copula. *Language* 45: 715-762.

Geoffrey Leech, Marianne Hundt, Christian Mair and Nicholas Smith. 2009. *Change in Contemporary English: a grammatical study*. Cambridge: Cambridge University Press.

Elena Lieven, Heike Behrens, Jennifer Speares and Michael Tomasello. 2003. Early syntactic creativity: a usage-based approach. *Journal of Child Language* 30: 333-370.

Luigi Rizzi. 1993/1994. Some notes on linguistic theory and language development: The case of root infinitives. *Language Acquisition* 3: 371-393.

Geoffrey Sampson. 2001. *Empirical Linguistics*. London: Continuum.

Anna Theakston, Elena Lieven, Julian Pine and Caroline Rowland. 2005. The acquisition of auxiliary syntax: BE and HAVE. *Cognitive Linguistics* 16: 247-277.

Harry Tily, Susanne Gahl, Inbal Arnon, Neal Snider, Anubha Kothari and Joan Bresnan. 2009. Syntactic probabilities affect pronunciation variation in spontaneous speech. *Language and Cognition* 1: 147-165.

Kenneth Wexler. 1994. Optional Infinitives, head movement and the economy of derivations. In: David Lightfoot and Norbert Hornstein (eds.), *Verb Movement*. Cambridge: Cambridge University Press.

Stephen Wilson. 2003. Lexically specific constructions in the acquisition of inflection in English. *Journal of Child Language* 30: 75-115.

Cross-lingual variation of light verb constructions: using parallel corpora and automatic alignment for linguistic research

Tanja Samardžić
Linguistics Department
University of Geneva
Tanja.Samardzic@unige.ch

Paola Merlo
Linguistics Department
University of Geneva
Paola.Merlo@unige.ch

Abstract

Cross-lingual parallelism and small-scale language variation have recently become subject of research in both computational and theoretical linguistics. In this article, we use a parallel corpus and an automatic aligner to study English light verb constructions and their German translations. We show that parallel corpus data can provide new empirical evidence for better understanding the properties of light verbs. We also study the influence that the identified properties of light verb constructions have on the quality of their automatic alignment in a parallel corpus. We show that, even though characterised by limited compositionality, these constructions can be aligned better than fully compositional phrases, due to an interaction between the type of light verb construction and its frequency.

1 Introduction

Fine-grained contrastive studies traditionally belong to the field of applied linguistics, notably to translation and second language acquisition studies. Recently, however, interest for contrastive studies has been renewed due to developments in the general theory of language (the notion of micro-parameters (Kayne, 2000)) on the one hand, and due to advances in natural language processing based on the exploitation of parallel corpora, on the other hand.

Parallel corpora are collections of translations with explicit alignment of sentences. They are important resources for the automatic acquisition of the cross-linguistic translation equivalents that are needed for machine translation. There is also interest in using parallel corpora to automatically develop new annotated linguistic resources by projecting the annotation that already exists in one language (usually English) (Padó, 2007; Basili et al., 2009). Such resources can be used for training systems for automatic parsing for different languages. Recently, parallel multilingual corpora have also been used to improve performance in mono-lingual tasks (Snyder et al., 2009).

For most of these applications, the aligned sentences in the parallel corpora need to be analysed into smaller units (phrases and words), which, in turn, need to be aligned. Although crucial for successful use of parallel corpora, word (and phrase) alignment is still a challenging task (Och and Ney, 2003; Collins et al., 2005; Padó, 2007).

Our research concentrates on one type of construction that needs a special treatment in the task of aligning corpora and projecting linguistic annotation from one language to another, namely light verb constructions. These constructions, usually identified as paraphrases of verbs (e.g. *have a laugh* means *laugh*, *give a talk* means *talk*), are frequent, cross-lingually productive forms, where simple-minded parallelism often breaks down. Their meaning is partially uncompositional, formed in a conventional way, which means that they cannot be analysed as regular constructions and that they cannot be translated to another language directly word by word. Unlike collocations and idioms, however, these constructions are formed according to the same "semi-productive" pattern in different languages. Due to their cross-lingual analysability, they can be expected to be aligned at the word level in a parallel corpus, even if their components are not direct word-to-word translations of each other. This means that word alignment of these constructions, needed for automatic translation and transferring annotations, is possible, but it is not straight-forward.

An in-depth study of these constructions in the specific context of parallel corpora and alignment can cast new light on the correlation of their linguistic and statistical properties. On the one hand,

Proceedings of the 2010 Workshop on NLP and Linguistics: Finding the Common Ground, ACL 2010, pages 52–60,
Uppsala, Sweden, 16 July 2010.

the statistical large-scale analysis of the behaviour of these constructions as the output of an alignment process provides novel linguistic information, which enlarges the empirical base for the analysis of these constructions, and complements the traditional grammaticality judgements. On the other hand, the linguistically fine-grained analysis of the statistical behaviour of these constructions provides linguistically-informed performance and error analyses that can be used to improve aligners.

2 Two Types of Light Verb Constructions and their Alignment

Light verb constructions have already been identified as one of the major sources of problems in transferring semantic annotation between languages as close as English and German (Burchardt et al., 2009). Light verb constructions introduce two kinds of divergences that can pose a problem for automatic word alignment. In the case of *true light verb constructions* (Kearns, 2002), English phrases such as *have a laugh, give [stg.] a wipe*, and *take a look* typically correspond to German single words, *lachen, wischen*, and *blicken* respectively. Such correspondences can be expected to result in actual parallel sentences where English verbs *have, give*, and *take* would be either aligned with the verbs *lachen, wischen*, and *blicken* respectively or would have no alignment at all. Such alignments are not common cases and can be expected to pose a problem to an automatic aligner.

Another type of divergence concerns *constructions with vague action verbs* (Kearns, 2002). In this case, English phrases such as *make an agreement, make a decision*, and *give a talk* correspond to German phrases *einen Vertrag schliessen, eine Entscheidung treffen*, and *einen Vortrag halten*, respectively. Parallel sentences containing these constructions should be aligned so that English nouns *agreement, decision*, and *talk* are aligned with German nouns *Vertrag, Entscheidung*, and *Vortrag*. At the same time, English verb *make* should be aligned with German *schliessen* in the first example, with *treffen* in the second, and *give* should be aligned with *halten* in the third example. Aligning the nouns should not pose any problem, since these alignments are direct lexical translations (c.f. (LEO, 2006 9) online dictionary, for example) and they can be expected to be aligned in many different sentences. However, aligning the verbs is necessarily more complicated, since they are not direct translations of each other and cannot be expected to be aligned in other contexts.[1]

However, the difference between the two types of light verb constructions is not clear cut. They are better seen as two ends of a continuum of verb usages with different degrees of verbs' lightness and different degrees of compositionality of the meaning of constructions. (Stevenson et al., 2004; Butt and Geuder, 2001; Grimshaw and Mester, 1988). Even though several English verbs have been identified as having light usages (e.g. *take, make, have, give, pay*), there has been little research on the influence that the properties of the heading light verb can have on the degree of semantic compositionality of the construction.

The purpose of the present research is to examine the German translation equivalents of the range of different English light verb constructions occurring in a parallel corpus and study the differential performance of a standard aligner on this language pair for these constructions.

3 Experiments

Our study is based on the assumption that the quality and bijectivity of the alignment are proportional to the corpus frequency and linguistic compositionality of the construction. Therefore, we identify two aspects of the alignment of these constructions as the relevant objects of study.

First, we quantify the amount and nature of correct word alignments for light verb constructions compared to regular verbs, as determined by human inspection. Given the described divergences between English and German, it can be expected that light verb constructions will be aligned with a single word more often than constructions headed by a regular verb. Assuming that the properties of the heading light verbs do influence semantic compositionality of the constructions, it can also be expected that light verb constructions headed by different verbs will be differently aligned to the German translations, constituting different types of constructions.

[1]Direct word-to-word English translations of *schliessen* listed in the LEO dictionary, for example, are: *infer, comprise, imply, close, close down, conclude, consummate, draw up, lock, shut, shutdown, sign off, quit*, while *make* is only listed within the phrase that is translation for this particular collocation. Similarly, English word translations for *treffen* are: *encounter, hook up, cross, get together, meet, meet up, hit, hurt, score, strike*, while *make* can only be found as a part of the phrase-to-phrase translations.

Second, we evaluate the quality of automatic word alignments of light verb constructions.

Current word alignment models are based on the assumption that the best word alignments are composed of the best word-to-word translations (as an effect of using Expectation-Maximisation for training). Factors in the translations that deviate from one-to-one alignments are often lexically specific (fertility) and require sufficient statistics. Because of the interaction of these properties of the alignment model and the semi-compositionality of light verb constructions, these constructions can be expected to pose a problem for automatic word alignment. Specifically, we expect lower overall quality of word alignment in the sentences containing light verb constructions than in the sentences that contain corresponding regular constructions.

As indicated, however, we also expect that the quality of automatic word alignment will be influenced by different distributional phenomena that are not necessarily related to the linguistic properties of parallel texts, in particular related to frequency of some of the components of the construction.

These predictions about the alignment of light verb constructions in English and German and their realisations in a corpus are examined in an experiment.

3.1 Materials and Methods

A random sample of instances of each of the defined types of construction was extracted from a large word-aligned parallel corpus and manually examined.

3.1.1 Corpus

The instances of the phrases were taken from the English-German portion of the Europarl corpus (Koehn, 2005) that contains the proceedings of the sessions held in 1999, irrespective of the source language and of the direction of translation. Before sampling, the corpus was word-aligned using GIZA++ (Och and Ney, 2003). Alignments were performed in both directions, with German as the target language and with English as the target language.

3.1.2 Word alignment using GIZA++

The program for automatic word alignment, GIZA++, has been developed within a system for automatic translation. It implements a series of statistical word-based translation models. In these models, word alignment is represented as a single-valued function, mapping each word in the target sentence to one word in the source sentence. To account for the fact that some target language words cannot be aligned with any source language word, a special empty word ("NULL") is introduced in the source sentence.

The definition of word alignment does not allow many-to-many mappings between the words of two languages, needed for representing alignment of non-compositional multi-word expressions. However, it allows aligning multiple words in one language to a single word in the other language, which is needed for successful alignment of English light verb constructions.

3.1.3 Sampling phrase instances

To study light verb constructions in a parallel corpus systematically, we group the instances of the constructions into two types: light verb constructions headed by the verb *take*, as an example of true light verb constructions, and those headed by the verb *make*, as an example of vague action verbs. We compare both types of light verb constructions to regular constructions headed by the verbs which are WordNet synonyms of the verb *make* (*create, produce, draw, fix, (re)construct, (re)build, establish*) with the same subcategorization frame.

We analyse three samples of the constructions, one for each of the types defined by the heading verb. Each sample contains 100 instances randomly selected from the word-aligned parallel corpus. The constructions are represented as ordered pairs of words, where the first word is the verb that heads the construction and the second is the noun that heads the verb's complement. Only the constructions where the complement is the direct object were included in the analysis.[2]

3.1.4 Data collection

The following data were collected for each occurrence of the English word pairs.

The word or words in the German sentence that are actual translation of the English words were identified. If either the English or German verb

[2]This means that constructions such as *take something into consideration* were not included. The only exception to this were the instances of the construction *take something into account*. This construction was included because it is used as a variation of *take account of something* with the same translations to German.

form included auxiliary verbs or modals, these were not considered. Only the lexical part of the forms were regarded as word translations.

We then determine the type of mapping between the translations. If the German translation of an English word pair includes two words too (e.g. take+decision ↔ Beschluss+fassen), this was marked as the "2-2" type. If German translation is a single word, the mapping was marked with "2-1". This type of alignment is further distinguished into "2-1N" and "2-1V". In the first subtype, the English construction corresponds to a German noun (e.g. initiative+taken ↔ Initiative). In the second subtype, the English construction corresponds to a German verb (e.g. take+look ↔ anschauen). In the cases where a translation shift occurs so that no translation can be found, the mapping is marked with "2-0".

We also collect the information on automatic alignment for each element of the English word pair for both alignment directions. These data were collected for the elements of English word pairs (verbs and nouns) separately. The alignment was assessed as "good" if the word was aligned with its actual translation, as "bad" if the word was aligned with some other word, and as "no align" if no alignment was found. Note that the "no align" label could only occur in the setting were English was the source language, since all the words in the sentence had to be aligned in the case where it was the target language.

For example, a record of an occurrence of the English construction "make+proposal" extracted from the bi-sentence in (1) [3] would contain the information given in (2).

(1) Target language German
EN: *He made a proposal.*
DE: *Er(1) hat(1) einen(3) Vorschlag(4) gemacht(3).*

Target language English
DE: *Er hat einen Vorschlag gemacht.*
EN: *He(1) made(5) a(3) proposal(4).*

(2) English instance: made + proposal
German alignment: Vorschlag + gemacht
Type of mapping: 2-2

[3]Glosses:
Er hat einen Vorschlag gemacht.
he has a proposal made
The numbers in the brackets in the target sentences indicate the position of the automatically aligned source word.

		English		
		LVC take	LVC make	Regular
German translation	$2 \rightarrow 2$	57	50	94
	$2 \rightarrow 1N$	8	18	2
	$2 \rightarrow 1V$	30	28	2
	$2 \rightarrow 0$	5	4	2
	Total	100	100	100

Table 1: Types of mapping between English constructions and their translation equivalents in German.

Automatic alignment, target German, noun: good, verb: no align
Automatic alignment, target English, noun: good, verb: good

4 Results

In this section, we present the results of the analyses of both correct (manual) and automatic alignment of the three types of constructions, pointing out the relevant asymmetries.

4.1 Results of Manual Alignment

Table 1 shows how many times each of the four types of mapping (2-2; 2-1N; 2-1V; 2-0) between English constructions and their German translation equivalents occurs in the sample.

We can see that the three types of constructions tend to be mapped to their German equivalents in different ways. First, both types of light verb constructions are mapped to a single German word much more often than the regular constructions (38 instances of light verb constructions with *take* and 46 instances of light verb constructions with *make* vs. only 4 instances of regular constructions.). Confirming our initial hypothesis, this result suggests that the difference between fully compositional phrases and light verb constructions in English can be described in terms of the degree of the "2-1" mapping to German translation equivalents.

An asymmetry can be observed concerning the two subtypes of the "2-1" mapping too. The German equivalent of an English construction is more often a verb if the construction is headed by the verb *take* (in 30 occurrences, that is 79% of the 2-1 cases) than if the construction is headed by the verb *make* (28 occurrences, 61% cases).

		DE	EN
LVCs with *take*	Both EN words	5	57
	EN noun	63	79
	EN verb	6	57
LVCs with *make*	Both EN words	5	40
	EN noun	58	58
	EN verb	6	52
Regular construction	Both EN words	26	42
	EN noun	68	81
	EN verb	32	47

Table 2: Well-aligned instances of LVCs with *take*, with *make*, and with regular constructions (out of 100), produced by an automatic alignment, in both alignment directions (target is indicated).

In the case where the German translation equivalent for an English construction is a verb, both components of the English construction are included in the corresponding German verb, the verbal category of the light verb and the lexical content of the nominal complement. These instances are less compositional, more specific and idiomatic (e.g. take+care ↔ kümmern, take+notice ↔ berücksichtigen).

On the other hand, English constructions that correspond to a German noun are more compositional, less idiomatic and closer to the regular verb usages (e.g. make+proposal ↔ Vorschlag, make+changes ↔ Korrekturen). The noun that is regarded as their German translation equivalent is, in fact, the equivalent of the nominal part of the construction, while the verbal part is simply omitted. This result suggests that English light verb constructions with *take* are less compositional than the light verb constructions with *make*.

4.2 Results on Automatic Alignment

We evaluate the quality of automatic alignment of light verb constructions in comparison with regular phrases taking into account two factors, the alignment direction and the frequency of the elements of the constructions. The results are presented in the next two sections.

4.2.1 Direction of Alignment

Table 2 shows how the quality of automatic alignment varies depending on the direction of alignment, as well as on the type of construction. Recall that more than one target word can be aligned to the same source word and all words of the target have to be aligned.

It can be noted that all the three types of constructions are better aligned if the target language is English. However, the difference in the quality is bigger in light verb constructions than in regular constructions, clearly because in this direction the multi-word property of the English light verb constructions can be represented. Both words are well aligned in light verb constructions with *take* in 57 cases and with *make* in 40 cases if the target languages is English, which is comparable with regular constructions (42 cases). However, if the target language is German, both types of light verb constructions are aligned well (both words) in only 5 cases, while regular constructions are well aligned in 26 cases.

Looking into the alignment of the elements of the constructions (verbs and nouns) separately, we can notice that nouns are generally better aligned than verbs for all the three types of constructions, and in both directions. However, this difference is not the same in all cases. The difference in the quality of alignment of nouns and verbs is the same in both alignment directions for regular constructions, but it is more pronounced in light verb constructions if German is the target. On the other hand, if English is the target, the difference is smaller in light verb construction than in regular phrases. These results suggest that the direction of alignment influences more the alignment of verbs than the alignment of nouns in general. This influence is much stronger in light verb constructions than in regular constructions.

Finally, our initial hypothesis that the quality of alignment of light verb constructions is lower than the quality of alignment of regular constructions has only been confirmed in the case where German is the target language (both words well aligned in 26 cases, compared to only 5 cases in both types of light verb constructions). Regular verbs are especially better aligned than light verbs in this case (32 : 6). However, if the target is English, the quality of alignment of regular constructions is similar to that of light verb constructions with *make* (42 and 40 good alignments respectively), while the constructions with *take* are aligned even better than the other two types (57 good alignments). These results suggest that the type of construction which is the least compositional and the most idiomatic of the three is best aligned if the direction of alignment suits its properties.

Frequency	*take* LVC	*make* LVC	Regular
Low	12	25	62
High	76	35	8

Table 3: The three types of constructions partitioned by the frequency of the complements in the sample.

		Well aligned					
Freq		*take* LVC		*make* LVC		Regular	
Low Freq	Both	4	33	8	32	21	34
	N	8	66	8	32	47	75
	V	4	33	12	48	53	85
High Freq	Both	47	62	18	51	4	50
	N	64	84	27	77	8	100
	V	58	76	18	51	4	50

Table 4: Counts and percentages of well-aligned instances of the three types of constructions in relation with the frequency of the complements in the sample. The percentages represent the number of well-aligned instances out of the overall number of instances within one frequency range. English is the target language.

4.2.2 Frequency

Since the quality of alignment of the three types of constructions proved different from what was expected in the case where English was the target language, we examine further the automatic alignment in this direction. In particular, we study its interaction with frequency.

The frequency of the nouns is defined as the number of occurrences in the sample. It ranges from 1 to 20 occurrences in the sample of 100 instances. The instances of the constructions were divided into three frequency ranges: instances containing nouns with 1 occurrence were considered as low frequency items; those containing nouns that occurred 5 and more times in the sample were considered as high frequency items; nouns occurring 2, 3, and 4 times were considered as medium frequency items. Only low and high frequency items were considered in this analysis.

Table 3 reports the number of instances belonging to different frequency ranges. It can be noted that light verb constructions with *take* exhibit a small number of low frequency nouns. The number of low frequency nouns increases in the constructions with *make* (25/100), and it is much bigger in regular constructions (62/100). The opposite is true for high frequency nouns (LVCs with *take*: 76/100, with *make*: 35/100, regular: 8/100). Such distribution of low/high frequency items reflects different collocational properties of the constructions. In the most idiomatic constructions (with *take*), lexical selection is rather limited which results in little variation. Verbs in regular constructions select for a wide range of different complements with little reoccurrence. Constructions with *make* can be placed between these two types.

Different trends in the quality of automatic alignment can be identified for the three types of constructions depending on the frequency range of the complement in the constructions, as shown in Table 4. The quality of alignment of both components of the constructions is comparable for all the three types of constructions in low frequency items (in 33% of instances of light verb constructions with *take*, 32% of light verb constructions with *make*, and 34% of regular constructions both the verb and the noun were well aligned). It is also improved in high frequency items in all the three types, compared to low frequency. However, the improvement is bigger in light verb constructions with *take* (62% well aligned cases) than in LVCs with *make* (51%) and in regular constructions (50%).[4]

Looking into the components of the constructions separately, we can notice interesting differences in the quality of automatic alignment of verbs. The proportion of well-aligned verbs increases with the frequency of their complements in light verb constructions with *take* (33% of low frequency items compared to 76% of high frequency items.) It stays almost the same in light verb constructions with *make* (48% of low frequency items and 51% of high frequency items), and it even decreases in regular items (85% of low frequency items compared to only 50% of high frequency items).

5 Discussion

The results reported in the previous section confirm both components of our first hypothesis (on the expected differences in cross-lingual mapping) and refine the conditions under which the second hypothesis (on the expected differences in the quality of automatic alignment) is true. We discuss

[4]Note that the high frequency regular items are represented with only 8 instances, which is why the trends might not be clear enough for this subtype.

these conclusions in detail here.

5.1 Manual Alignment

Recall that the first component of our first hypothesis indicated that it is expected that light verb constructions will be aligned with a single word more often than constructions headed by a regular verb.

The analysis of corpus data has shown that there is a clear difference between English regular phrases and light verb constructions in the way they are mapped to their translation equivalents in German. Regular constructions are mapped word-by-word, with the English verb being mapped to the German verb, and the English noun to the German noun. A closer look into the only 4 examples where regular constructions were mapped as "2-1" shows that this mapping is not due to the "lightness" of the verb. In two of these cases, it is the content of the verb that is translated, not that of the noun (produce+goods ↔ Produktion; establishes+rights ↔ legt). This never happens in light verb constructions.

On the other hand, light verb constructions are much more often translated with a single German word. In both subtypes of the "2-1" mapping of light verb constructions, it is the content of the nominal complement that is translated, not that of the verb. The noun is either transformed into a verb (take+look ↔ anschauen) or it is translated directly with the verb being omitted (take+initiative ↔ Initiative).

This difference provides empirical grounds for distinguishing between semantically full and semantically impoverished verbs, a task that is often difficult on the basis of syntactic tests, since they often exhibit the same syntactic properties.

The second component of the first hypothesis indicated that it was expected that the two types of light verb constructions be differently aligned.

The finding that English light verb constructions with *take* tend to be aligned more often with a single German verb and less often to a single German noun than the constructions with *make* justifies classifying the instances into the types based on the heading verb, which is not a common practice in the linguistic literature. It suggests that some semantic or lexical properties of these verbs can determine the type of the construction. More precisely, the meaning of the constructions with *take* can be regarded as less compositional than the meaning of the constructions with *make*. This difference is also supported by the findings of a preliminary study of Serbian translation equivalents of these constructions (Samardžić, 2008). English constructions with *take* tend to be translated with a single verb in Serbian, while the constructions with *make* are usually translated word-by-word. [5]

5.2 Automatic alignment

The second hypothesis conjectured that we would find lower overall quality of word alignment in the sentences containing light verb constructions than in the sentences that contain corresponding regular constructions. The findings of this research show that the interactions between alignment and types of constructions is actually more complicated than this simple hypothesis, in some expected and some unexpected ways. To summarise, we found, first, better alignment of regular constructions compared to light verb constructions only if the target language is German; second, overall, alignment if English is target is better than if German is target; and thirdly, we found a clear frequency by construction interaction in the quality of alignment.

The quality of automatic alignment of both regular constructions and light verb constructions interacts with the direction of alignment. First, the alignment is considerably better if the target language is English than if it is German, which confirms the findings of (Och and Ney, 2003). Second, the expected difference in the quality of alignment between regular constructions and light verb constructions has only been found in the direction of alignment with German as the target language, that is where the "2-1" mapping is excluded. However, the overall quality of alignment in this direction is lower than in the other.

This result could be expected, given the general morphological properties of the two languages, as well as the formalisation of the notion of word alignment used in the system for automatic alignment. According to this definition, multiple words in the target language sentence can be aligned with a single word in the source language sentence, but not the other way around. Since English is

[5]The difference in the level of semantic compositionality of the constructions with *take* and *make* could follow from some semantic properties of these verbs, such as different aspectual properties or argument structures. However, establishing such a relation would require a more systematic semantic study of light, as well as full lexical uses of these verbs.

a morphologically more analytical language than German, multiple English words often need to be aligned with a single German word (a situation allowed if English is the target but not if German is the target).

The phrases in (3) illustrate the two most common cases of such alignments. First, English tends to use functional words (the preposition *of* in (3a)), where German applies inflection (genitive suffixes on the article *des* and on the noun *Bananensektors* in (3b). Second, compounds are regarded as multiple words in English (*banana sector*), while they are single words in German (*Bananensektors*). This asymmetry explains both the fact that automatic alignment of all the three types of constructions is better when the target language is English and that the alignment of light verb constructions is worse than the alignment of regular phrases when it is forced to be expressed as one-to-one mapping, which occurs when German is the alignment target.

(3) a. the infrastructure of the banana sector
b. die Infrastruktur des Bananensektors

Practically, all these factors need to be taken into consideration in deciding which version of alignment should be taken, be it for evaluation or for application in other tasks such as automatic translation or annotation projection. The intersection of the two directions has been proved to provide most reliable automatic alignment (Padó, 2007; Och and Ney, 2003). However, it excludes, by definition, all the cases of potentially useful good alignments that are only possible in one direction of alignment.

Linguistically, the fact that the expected difference in the quality of alignment between regular constructions and light verb constructions has only been found in the direction where English constructions could not be aligned with single German words can be seen as another empirical indication of semantic impoverishment of light verbs in comparison with full lexical verbs.

Finally, we found an unexpected frequency by construction interaction (Table 4), which explains the finding that regular phrases are not better aligned than light verb constructions if English is the target language (opposite to our second hypothesis). This interaction, well known in language processing and acquisition, occurs in those cases where marked constructions are very frequent. In our case, the marked construction is the semi-compositional light verb construction with *take*, which has frequent noun complements. In this case, despite the non-regularity of the construction, alignment is performed well if the direction of alignment allows its mapping to a single word. Also, with respect to this phenomenon, the constructions with *take* behave more markedly than those with *make*.

What is especially interesting about these data is the fact that the alignment is different not just between light verb constructions and regular constructions, but also between the two types of light verb constructions. The constructions with *take* exhibit more consistent properties of irregular items, while the constructions with *make* can be positioned somewhere between irregular and regular items. This additionally confirms the claim that these two types of constructions differ in the level of semantic compositionality, providing a basis for an improvement in their linguistic account.

6 Conclusions and Future Work

In this paper we have proposed a contrastive study of light verb constructions based on data collected through alignments of parallel corpora. We have shown how a linguistically refined analysis can shed light on particularly difficult cases for an alignment program, a useful result for improving current statistical machine translation systems. We have also shown how properties and behaviours of these constructions that can be found only in large parallel corpora and through sophisticated computational tools can shed light on the linguistic nature of the constructions under study.

Much remains to be done, both in this general methodology and for this particular kind of construction. As an example, we note that the fact that nouns are aligned better than verbs in all the three types of constructions deserves more investigation. What we do not yet know is whether this fact can be related to some known distributional differences between these two classes or not. It might also mean that nominal lexical items are more stable across languages than verbal ones. This can have implications for machine translations, as well as for annotation projection, since the stable words can be used as pivots for alignment and transfer algorithms.

References

Roberto Basili, Diego De Cao, Danilo Croce, Bonaventura Coppola, and Alessandro Moschitti. 2009. Cross-language frame semantics transfer in bilingual corpora. In Alexander F. Gelbukh, editor, *Proceedengs of the 10th International Conference on Intelligent Text Processing and Computational Linguistics*, pages 332–345, Mexico City, Mexico. Springer.

Aljoscha Burchardt, Katrin Erk, Anette Frank, Andrea Kowalski, Sebastian Padó, and Manfred Pinkal. 2009. FrameNet for the semantic analysis of German: Annotation, representation and automation. In Hans Boas, editor, *Multilingual FrameNets in Computational Lexicography: Methods and applications*, pages 209–244. Mouton de Gruyter.

Miriam Butt and Wilhelm Geuder. 2001. On the (semi)lexical status of light verbs. In Norbert Corver and Henk van Riemsdijk, editors, *Semilexical Categories: On the content of function words and the function of content words*, pages 323–370, Berlin. Mouton de Gruyter.

Michael Collins, Philipp Koehn, and Ivona Kučerová. 2005. Clause restructuring for statistical machine translation. In *Proceedings of the Annual Meeting of the Association for Computational Linguistics (ACL)*, pages 531–540, Ann Arbor. Association for Computational Linguistics.

Jane Grimshaw and Armin Mester. 1988. Light verbs and theta-marking. *Linguistic Inquiry*, 19:205–232.

Richard Kayne. 2000. *Parameters and Universals*. Oxford University Press, New York.

Kate Kearns. 2002. Light verbs in English. Manuscript.

Philipp Koehn. 2005. Europarl: A parallel corpus for statistical machine translation. In *Proceedings of MT Summit 2005*, Phuket, Thailand.

LEO. 2006-9. *LEO Online Dictionary*. LEO DictionaryTeam, http://dict.leo.org.

Franz Josef Och and Hermann Ney. 2003. A systematic comparison of various statistical alignment models. *Computational Linguistics*, 29(1):19–52.

Sebastian Padó. 2007. *Cross-Lingual Annotation Projection Models for Role-Semantic Information*. Ph.D. thesis, Saarland University.

Tanja Samardžić. 2008. Light verb constructions in English and Serbian. In *English Language and Literature Studies — Structures across Cultures*, pages 59–73, Belgrade. Faculty of Philology.

Benjamin Snyder, Tahira Naseem, Jacob Eisenstein, and Regina Barzilay. 2009. Adding more languages improves unsupervised multilingual part-of-speech tagging: a Bayesian non-parametric approach. In *Proceedings of Human Language Technologies: The 2009 Annual Conference of the North American Chapter of the Association for Computational Linguistics*, pages 83–91, Boulder, Colorado, June. Association for Computational Linguistics.

Suzanne Stevenson, Afsaneh Fazly, and Ryan North. 2004. Statistical measures of the semiproductivity of light verb constructions. In *Proceedings of the ACL04 Workshop on Multiword Expressions: Integrating Processing*, pages 1–8. Association for Computational Linguistics.

No sentence is too confusing to ignore

Paul Cook
Department of Computer Science
University of Toronto
Toronto, Canada
pcook@cs.toronto.edu

Suzanne Stevenson
Department of Computer Science
University of Toronto
Toronto, Canada
suzanne@cs.toronto.edu

Abstract

We consider sentences of the form *No X is too Y to Z*, in which X is a noun phrase, Y is an adjective phrase, and Z is a verb phrase. Such constructions are ambiguous, with two possible (and opposite!) interpretations, roughly meaning either that "Every X Zs", or that "No X Zs". The interpretations have been noted to depend on semantic and pragmatic factors. We show here that automatic disambiguation of this pragmatically complex construction can be largely achieved by using features of the lexical semantic properties of the verb (i.e., *Z*) participating in the construction. We discuss our experimental findings in the context of construction grammar, which suggests a possible account of this phenomenon.

1 No noun is too adjective to verb

Consider the following two sentences:

(1) No interest is too narrow to deserve its own newsletter.

(2) No item is too minor to escape his attention.

Each of these sentences has the form of *No X is too Y to Z*, where X, Y, and Z are a noun phrase, adjective phrase, and verb phrase, respectively. Sentence (1) is generally taken to mean that *every* interest deserves its own newsletter, regardless of how narrow it is. On the other hand, (2) is typically interpreted as meaning that *no* item escapes his attention, regardless of how minor it is. That is, sentences with the identical form of *No X is too Y to Z* either can mean that "*every* X Zs", or can mean the opposite—that "*no* X Zs"![1]

This "verbal illusion" (Wason and Reich, 1979), so-called because there are two opposite interpretations for the very same structure, is of interest to us for two reasons. First, the contradictory nature of the possible meanings has been explained in terms of pragmatic factors concerning the relevant presuppositions of the sentences. According to Wason and Reich (1979) (as explained in more detail below), sentences such as (2) are actually nonsensical, but people coerce them into a sensible reading by reversing the interpretation. One of our goals in this work is to explore whether computational linguistic techniques—specifically automatic corpus analysis drawing on lexical resources—can help to elucidate the factors influencing interpretation of such sentences across a collection of actual usages.

The second reason for our interest in this construction is that it illustrates a complex ambiguity that can cause difficulty for natural language processing applications that seek to semantically interpret text. Faced with the above two sentences, a parsing system (in the absence of specific knowledge of this construction) will presumably find the exact same structure for each, giving no basis on which to determine the correct meaning from the parse. (Unsurprisingly, when we run the C&C Parser (Curran et al., 2007) on (1) and (2) it assigns the same structure to each sentence.) Our second goal in this work is thus to explore whether increased linguistic understanding of this phenomenon could be used to disambiguate such examples automatically. Specifically, we use this construction as an example of the kind of difficulties faced in semantic interpretation when meaning may be determined by pragmatic or other extra-syntactic factors, in order to explore whether

[1]Note that in examples (1) and (2), the nouns *interest* and *item* are the subjects of the verbs *deserve* and *escape*, respectively. In this construction the noun can also be the object of the verb, as in the title of this paper which claims no sentence can/should be ignored.

Proceedings of the 2010 Workshop on NLP and Linguistics: Finding the Common Ground, ACL 2010, pages 61–69,
Uppsala, Sweden, 16 July 2010.

lexical semantic features can be used as cues to resolving pragmatic ambiguity when a complex semantico-pragmatic model is not feasible.

In the remainder of this paper, we present the first computational study of the *No X is too Y to Z* phenomenon, which attempts to automatically determine the meaning of instances of this semantically and pragmatically complex construction. In Section 2 we present previous analyses of this construction, and our hypothesis. In Section 3, we describe the creation of a dataset of instances that verifies that both interpretations ("every" and "no") indeed occur in corpora. We then analyze the human annotations in this dataset in more detail in Section 4. In Section 5, we present the feature model we use to describe the instances, which taps into the lexical semantics and polarity of the constituents. In Section 6, we describe machine learning experiments and classification results that support our hypothesis that the interpretation of this construction largely depends on the semantics of its component verb. In Section 7 we suggest that our results support an analysis of this phenomenon within construction grammar, and point to some future directions in our research in Section 8.

2 Background and our proposal

The *No X is too Y to Z* construction was investigated by Wason and Reich (1979), and discussed more recently by Pullum (2004) and Liberman (2009a,b). Here we highlight some of the most important properties of this complex phenomenon. Our presentation owes much to the lucid discussion and clarification of this topic, and of the work of Wason and Reich specifically, by Liberman.

Wason and Reich argue that the compositional interpretation of sentences of the form of (1) and (2) is "every X Zs". Intuitively, this can be understood by considering a sentence identical to sentence (1), but without a negative subject: *This interest is too narrow to deserve its own newsletter*, which means that "this interest is so narrow that it does not deserve a newsletter". This example indicates that the meaning of *too narrow to deserve its own newsletter* is "so narrow that it does not deserve a newsletter". When this negative "too" assertion is compositionally combined with the *No interest* subject of sentence (1), it results in a meaning with two negatives: "No interest is so narrow that it does not deserve a newsletter", or simply, "Every interest deserves a newsletter". Wason and Reich note that in sentences such as (1), the compositional "every" interpretation is consistent with common beliefs about the world, and thus refer to such sentences as "pragmatic".

By contrast, the compositional interpretation of sentences such as (2) does not correspond to our common sense beliefs. Consider an analogous (non-negative subject) sentence to sentence (2)—i.e., *This item is too minor to escape his attention.* It is nonsensical that "This item is so minor that it does not escape his attention", since being more "minor" entails more likelihood of escaping attention, not less. The compositional interpretation of (2) is similarly nonsensical—i.e., that "No item is so minor that it does not escape his attention"; Such sentences are thus termed "non-pragmatic" by Wason and Reich, who argue that the complexity of the non-pragmatic sentences—arising in part due to the number of negations they contain—causes the listener or reader to misconstrue them. According to their reasoning, listeners choose an interpretation that is consistent with their beliefs about the world—namely that "no X Zs", in this case that "No item escapes his attention"—instead of the compositional interpretation ("Every item escapes his attention").

While Wason and Reich focus on the compositional semantics and pragmatics of these sentences, they also note that the non-pragmatic examples typically use a verb that itself has some aspect of negation, such as *ignore*, *miss*, and *overlook*. This property is also pointed out by Pullum (2004), who notes that *avoid* in his example of the construction means "manage to **not** do" something. Building on this observation, we hypothesize that lexical properties of the component constituents of this construction, particularly the verb, can be important cues to its semantico-pragmatic interpretation. Specifically, we hypothesize that the pragmatic ("every" interpretation) and non-pragmatic ("no" interpretation) sentences will tend to involve verbs with different semantics. Given that verbs of different semantic classes have different selectional preferences, we also expect to see the "every" and "no" sentences associated with semantically different nouns and adjectives.

3 Dataset

3.1 Extraction

To create a dataset of usages of the construction *no NP is too AP to VP*—referred to as the target construction—we use two corpora: the British National Corpus (Burnard, 2000), an approximately one hundred million word corpus of late-twentieth century British English, and The New York Times Annotated Corpus (Sandhaus, 2008), approximately one billion words of non-newswire text from the New York Times from the years 1987–2006. We extract all sentences in these corpora containing the sequence of strings *no*, *is too*, and *to* separated by one or more words. We then manually filter all sentences that do not have *no NP* as the subject of *is too*, or that do not have *to VP* as an argument of *is too*. After removing duplicates, this results in 170 sentences. We randomly select 20 of these sentences for development data, leaving 150 sentences for testing.

Although we find only 170 examples of the target construction in 1.1 billion words of text, note that our extraction process is quite strict and misses some relevant usages. For example, we do not extract sentences of the form *Nothing is too Y to Z* in which the subject NP does not contain the word *no*. Nor do we extract usages of the related construction *No X is too Y for Z*, where Z is an NP related to a verb, as in *No interest is too narrow for attention*. (We would only extract the latter if there were an infinitive verb embedded in or following the NP.) In the present study we limit our consideration to sentences of the form discussed by Wason and Reich (1979), but intend to consider related constructions such as these—which appear to exhibit the same ambiguity as the target construction—in the future.

We next manually identify the noun, adjective, and verb that participate in the target construction in each sentence. Although this could be done automatically using a parser (e.g., Collins, 2003) or chunker (e.g., Abney, 1991), here we want to ensure error-free identification. We also note a number of sentences containing co-ordination, such as in the following example.

(3) These days, no topic is too recent or specialized to disqualify it from museum apotheosis.

This sentence contains two instances of the target construction: one corresponding to the noun-adjective-verb triple *topic*, *recent*, *disqualify*, and the other to the triple *topic*, *specialized*, *disqualify*. In general, we consider each unique noun-adjective-verb triple participating in the target construction as a separate instance.

3.2 Annotation

We used Amazon Mechanical Turk (AMT, `https://www.mturk.com/`) to obtain judgements as to the correct interpretation of each instance of the target construction in both the development and testing datasets. For each instance, we generated two paraphrases, one corresponding to each of the interpretations discussed in Section 1. We then presented the given instance of the target construction along with its two paraphrases to annotators through AMT, as shown in Table 1. In generating the paraphrases, one of the authors selected the most appropriate paraphrase, in their judgement, where *can* in the paraphrases in Table 1 was selected from *can*, *should*, *will*, and $\emptyset$. Note that the paraphrases do not contain the adjective from the target construction. In the case of multiple instances of the target construction with differing adjectives but the same noun and verb, we only solicited judgements for one instance, and used these judgements for the other instances. In our dataset we observe that all instances obtained from the same sentence which differ only with respect to their noun or verb have the same interpretation. We therefore believe that instances with the same noun and verb but a different adjective are unlikely to differ in their interpretation.

Instructions:

- Read the sentence below.
- Based on your interpretation of that sentence, select the answer that most closely matches your interpretation.
- Select "I don't know" if neither answer is close to your interpretation, or if you are really unsure.

That success was accomplished in large part to tight control on costs , and no cost is too small to be scrutinized .

- Every cost can be scrutinized.
- No cost can be scrutinized.
- I don't know.

Enter any feedback you have about this HIT. We greatly appreciate you taking the time to do so.

Table 1: A sample of the Amazon Mechanical Turk annotation task.

We also allowed the judges to optionally enter any feedback about the annotation task which in some cases—discussed in the following section—was useful in determining whether the judges found a particular instance difficult to annotate.[2]

For each instance of the target construction we obtained three judgements from unique workers on AMT. For approximately 80% of the items, the judgements were unanimous. In the remaining cases we solicited four additional judgements, and used the majority judgement. We paid $0.05 per judgement; the average time spent on each annotation was approximately twenty seconds, resulting in an average hourly wage of about $10.

The development data was also annotated by three native English speaking experts (computational linguists with extensive linguistic background, two of whom are also authors of this paper). The inter-annotator agreement among these judges is very high, with pairwise observed agreements of 1.00, 0.90, and 0.90, and corresponding unweighted Kappa scores of 1.00, 0.79, and 0.79. The majority judgements of these annotators are the same as those obtained from AMT on the development data, giving us confidence in the reliability of the AMT judgements. These findings are consistent with those of Snow et al. (2008) in showing that AMT judgements can be as reliable as those of expert judges.

Finally, we remove a small number of items from the testing dataset which were difficult to paraphrase due to ellipsis of the verb participating in the target construction, or an extra negation in the verb phrase. We further remove one sentence because we believe the paraphrases we provided are in fact misleading. The number of sentences and of instances (i.e., noun-verb-adjective triples) of the target construction in the development and testing datasets is given in Table 2. 160 of the 199 testing instances (80%) have the "every" interpretation, with the remainder having the "no" interpretation.

4 Analysis of annotation

We now more closely examine the annotations obtained from AMT to better determine the extent to which they are reliable. We also consider specific instances of the target construction that are judged inconsistently to establish some of the causes of disagreement.

Dataset	# sentences	# instances
Development	20	33
Test	140	199

Table 2: The number of sentences containing the target construction, and the number of resulting instances.

One of the three experts who annotated the development items (discussed in Section 3.2) also annotated twenty items selected at random from the testing data. In this case two instances are judged differently than the majority judgement obtained from AMT. These instances are given below with the noun, adjective and verb in the target construction underlined.

(4) When it comes to the clash of candidates on national television, no detail, it seems, is too minor for negotiation, no risk too small to eliminate.

(5) Lectures by big-name Wall Street felons will show why no swindler is too big to beat the rap by peaching on small-timers.

For sentence (4), the AMT judgements were unanimously for the "no" interpretation whereas the expert annotator chose the "every" interpretation. We are uncertain as to the reason for this disagreement, but are convinced that the "every" interpretation is the intended one.

In the case of sentence (5), the AMT judgements were split four–three for the "every" and "no" interpretations, respectively, while the expert annotator chose the "no" interpretation. For this sentence the provided paraphrases were *Every swindler can beat the rap* and *No swindler can beat the rap.* If attention in the sentence is restricted to the target construction—i.e., *no swindler is too big to beat the rap by peaching on small-timers*—either of the "no" and "every" interpretations is possible. That is, this clause alone can mean that "no swindler is 'big' enough to be able to beat the rap" (the "no" interpretation), or that "no swindler is 'big' enough that they

[2]In other cases the comments were more humourous. In response to the following sentence *If you've ever yearned to live on Sesame Street, where no problem is too big to be solved by a not-too-big slice of strawberry-rhubarb pie, this is the spot for you,* one judge told us her preferred types of pie.

are above peaching on small-timers" (or in other words, "every swindler is able to beat the rap by peaching on small-timers", the "every" interpretation). However, the intention of the sentence as the "no" interpretation is clear from the referral in the main clause to *big-name Wall Street felons*, which implies that "big" swindlers have *not* beaten the rap. Since the AMT annotators may not be devoting a large amount of attention to the task, they may focus only on the target construction and not the preliminary disambiguating material. In this event, they may be choosing between the "every" and "no" interpretations based on how cynical they are of the ability (or lack thereof) of the American legal system to punish Wall Street criminals.

We also examine a small number of examples in the testing set which do not receive a clear majority judgement from AMT. For this analysis we consider items for which the difference in the number of judgements for each of the "every" and the "no" interpretations is one or less This gives four instances of the target construction, one of which we have already discussed above, example (5); the others are presented below, again with the noun, adjective, and verb participating in the target construction underlined:

(6) Where are our priorities when we so carefully weigh costs and medical efficacy in deciding to offer a medical lifeline to the elderly, yet no amount of money is too great to spend on the debatable paths we've taken in our war against terror?

(7) No neighborhood is too remote to diminish Mr. Levine's determination to discover and announce some previously unheralded treat.

(8) No one is too remote anymore to be concerned about style, Ms. Hansen suggested.

In example (6) the author is using the target construction to express somebody else's viewpoint that "any amount should be spent on the war against terror". Therefore the literal reading of the target construction appears to be the "every" interpretation. However, this construction is being used rhetorically (as part of the overall sentence) to express the author's belief that "too much money is being spent on the war against terror", which is close in meaning to the "no" interpretation. It appears that the annotators are split between these two readings. For sentence (7) the atypicality of *neighbourhood* as the subject of *diminish* may make this instance particularly difficult for the judges. Sentence (8) appears to us to be a clear example of the "every" interpretation. The paraphrases for this usage are "Everyone should be concerned about style" and "No one should be concerned about style". In this case it is possible that the judges are biased by their beliefs about whether one should be concerned about style, and that this is giving rise to the lack of agreement. These examples illustrate that some of these usages are clearly complex for people to annotate. Such complex examples may require more context to be annotated with confidence.

5 Model

To test our hypothesis that the interaction of the semantics of the noun, adjective, and verb in the target construction contributes to its pragmatic interpretation, we represent each instance in our dataset as a vector of features that capture aspects of the semantics of its component words.

WordNet To tap into general lexical semantic properties of the words in the construction, we use features that draw on the semantic classes of words in WordNet (Fellbaum, 1998). These binary features each represent a synset in WordNet, and are turned on or off for the component words (the noun, adjective, and verb) in each instance of the target construction. A synset feature is on for a word if the synset occurs on the path from all senses of the word to the root, and off otherwise. We use WordNet version 3.0 accessed using NLTK version 2.0 (Bird et al., 2009).

Polarity Because of the observation that the verb in the target construction, in particular, has some property of negativity in the "no" interpretation, we also use features representing the semantic polarity of the noun, adjective, and verb in each instance. The features are tertiary, representing positive, neutral, or negative polarity. We obtain polarity information from the subjectivity lexicon provided by Wilson et al. (2005), and consider words to be neutral if they have both positive and negative polarity, or are not in the lexicon.

6 Experimental results

6.1 Experimental setup

To evaluate our model we conduct a 5-fold cross-validation experiment using the items in the testing dataset. When partitioning the items in the testing dataset into the five parts necessary for the cross-validation experiment, we ensure that all the instances of the target construction from a single sentence are in the same part. This ensures that no instance used for training is from the same sentence as an instance used for testing. We further ensure that the proportion of items in each class is roughly the same in each split.

For each of the five runs, we linearly scale the training data to be in the range $[-1, 1]$, and apply the same transformation to the testing data. We train a support vector machine (LIBSVM version 2.9, Chang and Lin, 2001) with a radial basis function kernel on the training portion in each run, setting the cost and gamma parameters using cross-validation on just the training portion, and then test the classifier on the testing portion for that run using the same parameter settings. We micro-average the accuracy obtained on each of the five runs. Finally, we repeat each 5-fold cross-validation experiment five times, with five random splits, and report the average accuracy over these trials.

6.2 Results

Results for experiments using various subsets of the features are presented in Table 3. We restrict the component word—the noun, adjective, or verb—for which we extract features to those listed in column "Word", and extract only the features given in column "Features" (WordNet, polarity, or all). The majority baseline is 80%, corresponding to always selecting the "every" interpretation. Accuracies shown in boldface are significantly better than the majority class baseline using a paired t-test. (In all cases where the difference is significant, we obtain $p \ll 0.01$.)

We first consider the results using features extracted only for the noun, adjective, or verb individually, using all features. The best accuracy in this group of experiments, 87%, is achieved using the verb features, and is significantly higher than the majority baseline. On the other hand, the classifiers trained on the noun and adjective features individually perform no better than the baseline. These results support our hypothesis that lexical semantic properties of the component verb in the *No X is too Y to Z* construction do indeed play an important role in determining its interpretation. Although we proposed that selectional constraints from the verb would also lead to differing semantics of the nouns and adjectives in the two interpretations, our WordNet features are likely too simplistic to capture this effect, if it does hold. Before ruling out the semantic contribution of these words to the interpretation, we need to explore whether a more sophisticated model of selectional preferences, as in Ciaramita and Johnson (2000) or Clark and Weir (2002), yields more informative features for the noun and adjective.

Experimental setup		% accuracy
Word	Features	
Noun	All	80
Adjective	All	80
Verb	All	**87**
All	WordNet	**88**
All	Polarity	80
All	All	**88**
Majority baseline		80

Table 3: % accuracy on testing data for each experimental condition and the majority baseline. Accuracies in boldface are statistically significantly different from the baseline.

We now consider the results using the WordNet and polarity features individually, but extracted for all three component words. The WordNet features perform as well as the best results using all features for all three words, which gives further support to our hypothesis that the semantics of the components of the target construction are related to its interpretation. The polarity features perform poorly. This is perhaps unsurprising as polarity is a poor approximation to the property of "negativity" that we are attempting to capture. Moreover, many of the nouns, adjectives, and verbs in our dataset either have neutral polarity or are not in the polarity lexicon, and therefore the polarity features are not very discriminative. In future work, we plan to examine the WordNet classes of the verbs that occur in the "no" interpretation to try to more precisely characterize the property of negativity that these verbs tend to have.

6.3 Error analysis

To better understand the errors our classifier is making, we examine the specific instances which are classified incorrectly. Here we focus on the experiment using all features for all three component words. There are 23 instances which are consistently mis-classified in all runs of the experiment. According to the AMT judgements, each of these instances corresponds to the "no" interpretation. These errors reflect the bias of the classifier towards the more frequent class, the "every" interpretation.

We further note that two of the instances discussed in Section 4—examples (4) and (6)—are among those instances consistently classified incorrectly. The majority judgement from AMT for both of these instances is the "no" interpretation, while in our assessment they are in fact the "every" interpretation. We are therefore not surprised to see these items "mis-classified" as "every".

Example (8) was incorrectly classified in one trial. In this case we agree with the gold-standard label obtained from AMT in judging this instance as the "every" interpretation; nevertheless, this does appear to be a difficult instance given the low agreement observed for the AMT judgements.

It is interesting that no items with an "every" interpretation are consistently misclassified. In the context of our overall results showing the impact of the verb features on performance, we conclude that the "no" interpretation arises due to particular lexical semantic properties of certain verbs. We suspect then that the consistent errors on the 21 truly misclassified expressions (23 minus the 2 instances discussed above that we believe to be annotated incorrectly) are due to sparse data. That is, if it is indeed the verb that plays a major role in leading to a "no" interpretation, there may simply be insufficient numbers of such verbs for training a supervised model in a dataset with only 39 examples of those usages.

7 Discussion

We have presented the first computational study of the semantically and pragmatically complex construction *No X is too Y to Z*. We have developed a computational model that automatically disambiguates the construction with an accuracy of 88%, reducing the error-rate over the majority-baseline by 40%. The model uses features that tap into the lexical semantics of the component words participating in the construction, particularly the verb. These results demonstrate that lexical properties can be successful in resolving an ambiguity previously thought to depend on complex pragmatic inference over presuppositions (as in Wason and Reich (1979)).

These results can be usefully situated within the context of linguistic and psycholinguistic work on semantic interpretation processing. Beginning around 20 years ago, work in modeling of human semantic preferences has focused on the extent to which properties of lexical items influence the interpretation of various linguistic ambiguities (e.g., Trueswell and Tanenhaus, 1994). While semantic context and plausibility are also proposed to play a role in human interpretation of ambiguous sentences (e.g., Crain and Steedman, 1985; Altmann and Steedman, 1988), it has been pointed out that it would be difficult to "operationalize" the complex interactions of presuppositional factors with real-world knowledge in a precise algorithm for disambiguation (Jurafsky, 1996). Although not intended as proposing a cognitive model, the work here can be seen as connected to these lines of research, in investigating the extent to which lexical factors can be used as proxies to more "hidden" features that underlie the appropriate interpretation of a pragmatically complex construction.

Moreover, as in the approach of Jurafsky (1996), the phenomenon we investigate here may be best considered within a constructional analysis (e.g., Langacker, 1987), in which both the syntactic construction and the particular lexical items contribute to the determination of the meaning of a usage. We suggest that a clause of the form *No X is too Y to Z* might be the (identical) surface expression of *two* underlying constructions—one with the "every" interpretation and one with the "no" interpretation—which place differing constraints on the semantics of the verb. (E.g., in the "no" interpretation, the verb typically has some "negative" semantic property, as noted in Section 2.) Looked at from the other perspective, the lexical semantic properties of the verb might determine which *No X is too Y to Z* construction (and associated interpretation) it is compatible with. Our results support this view, by showing that semantic classes of verbs have predictive value in selecting the correct interpretation.

Note that such a constructional analysis of this phenomenon assumes that both interpretations of these sentences are linguistically valid, given the appropriate lexical instantiation. This stands in contrast to the analysis of Wason and Reich (1979), which presumes that people are applying some higher-level reasoning to "correct" an ill-formed statement in the case of the "no" interpretation. While such extra-grammatical inference may play a role in support of language understanding when people are faced with noisy data, it seems unlikely to us that a construction that is used quite readily and with a predictable interpretation is nonsensical according to rules of grammar. Our results point to an alternative linguistic analysis, one whose further development may also help to improve automatic disambiguation of instances of *No X is too Y to Z*. In the next section, we discuss directions for future work that could elaborate on these preliminary findings.

8 Future Work

One limitation of this study is that the dataset used is rather small, consisting of just 199 instances of the target construction. As discussed in Section 3.1, the extraction process we use to obtain our experimental items has low recall; in particular it misses variants of the target construction such as *Nothing is too Y to Z* and *No X is too Y for Z*. In the future we intend to expand our dataset by extracting such usages. Furthermore, the data used in the present study is primarily taken from news text. While we do not adopt the view of some that usages of the target construction having the "no" interpretation are errors, it could be the case that such usages are more frequent in less formal text. In the future we also intend to extract usages of the target construction from datasets of less formal text, such as blogs (e.g., Burton et al., 2009).

Constructions other than *No X is too Y to Z* exhibit a similar ambiguity. For example, the construction *X didn't wait to Y* is ambiguous between "X did Y right away" and "X didn't do Y at all" (Karttunen, 2007). In the future we would like to extend our study to consider more such constructions which are ambiguous due to the interpretation of negation.

In Section 4 we note that for some instances the complexity of the sentences containing the target construction may make it difficult for the annotators to judge the meaning of the target. In the future we intend to present simplified versions of these sentences—which retain the noun, adjective, and verb from the target construction in the original sentence—to the judges to avoid this issue. Such an approach will also help us to focus more clearly on observable lexical semantic effects.

We are particularly interested in further exploring the hypothesis that it is the semantics of the component verb that gives rise to the meaning of the target construction. Recall Pullum's (2004) observation that the verb in the "no" interpretation involves explicitly *not* acting. Using this intuition, we have informally observed that it is largely possible to (manually) predict the interpretation of the target construction knowing only the component verb. We are interested in establishing the extent to which this observation holds, and precisely which aspects of a verb's meaning give rise to the interpretation of the target construction.

Our current model of the semantics of the target construction does not capture Wason and Reich's (1979) observation that the compositional meaning of instances having the "no" interpretation is non-pragmatic. While we do not adopt their view that these usages are somehow "errors", we do think that their observation can indicate other possible lexical semantic properties that may help to identify the correct interpretation. Taking the classic example from Wason and Reich, *no head injury is too trivial to ignore*, one clue to the "no" interpretation is that generally a head injury is not something that is ignored. On the other hand, considering Wason and Reich's example *no missile is too small to ban*, it is widely believed that missiles should be banned. We would like to add features that capture this knowledge to our model.

In preliminary experiments we have used co-occurrence information as an approximation to this knowledge. (For example, we would expect that *head injury* would tend to co-occur less with *ignore* than with antonymous verbs such as *treat* or *address*.) Although our early results using co-occurrence features do not indicate that they are an improvement over the other features considered (WordNet and polarity), it may also be the case that our present formulation of these co-occurrence features does not effectively capture the intended knowledge. In the future we plan to further consider such features, especially those that model the selectional preferences of the verb participating in the target construction.

These several strands of future work—increasing the size of the dataset, improving the quality of annotation, and exploring additional features in our computational model—will enable us to extend our linguistic analysis of this interesting phenomenon, as well as to improve performance on automatic disambiguation of this complex construction.

Acknowledgments

We thank Magali Boizot-Roche and Timothy Fowler for their help in preparing the data for this study. This research was financially supported by the Natural Sciences and Engineering Research Council of Canada and the University of Toronto.

References

Steven Abney. 1991. Parsing by chunks. In Robert Berwick, Steven Abney, and Carol Tenny, editors, *Principle-Based Parsing: Computation and Psycholinguistics*, pages 257–278. Kluwer Academic Publishers.

Gerry T. M. Altmann and Mark Steedman. 1988. Interaction with context during human sentence processing. *Cognition*, 30(3):191–238.

Steven Bird, Edward Loper, and Ewan Klein. 2009. *Natural Language Processing with Python*. O'Reilly Media Inc.

Lou Burnard. 2000. *The British National Corpus Users Reference Guide*. Oxford University Computing Services.

Kevin Burton, Akshay Java, and Ian Soboroff. 2009. The ICWSM 2009 Spinn3r Dataset. In *Proc. of the Third International Conference on Weblogs and Social Media*. San Jose, CA.

Chih-Chung Chang and Chih-Jen Lin. 2001. *LIBSVM: a library for support vector machines*. Software available at `http://www.csie.ntu.edu.tw/~cjlin/libsvm`.

Massimiliano Ciaramita and Mark Johnson. 2000. Explaining away ambiguity: Learning verb selectional preference with Bayesian networks. In *Proceedings of the 18th International Conference on Computational Linguistics (COLING 2000)*, pages 187–193. Saarbrücken, Germany.

Stephen Clark and David Weir. 2002. Class-based probability estimation using a semantic hierarchy. *Computational Linguistics*, 28(2):187–206.

Michael Collins. 2003. Head-driven statistical models for natural language parsing. *Computational Linguistics*, 29(4):589–637.

Stephen Crain and Mark Steedman. 1985. On not being led up the garden path: The use of context by the psychological syntax processor. In David R. Dowty, Lauri Karttunen, and Arnold M. Zwicky, editors, *Natural language parsing: Psychological, computational, and theoretical perspectives*, pages 320–358. Cambridge University Press, Cambridge.

James Curran, Stephen Clark, and Johan Bos. 2007. Linguistically motivated large-scale NLP with C&C and Boxer. In *Proceedings of the 45th Annual Meeting of the Association for Computational Linguistics Companion Volume Proceedings of the Demo and Poster Sessions*, pages 33–36. Prague, Czech Republic.

Christiane Fellbaum, editor. 1998. *Wordnet: An Electronic Lexical Database*. Bradford Books.

Daniel Jurafsky. 1996. A probabilistic model of lexical and syntactic access and disambiguation. *Cognitive Science*, 20(2):137–194.

Lauri Karttunen. 2007. Word play. *Computational Linguistics*, 33(4):443–467.

Ronald W. Langacker. 1987. *Foundations of Cognitive Grammar: Theoretical Prerequisites*, volume 1. Stanford University Press, Stanford.

Mark Liberman. 2009a. No detail too small. Retrieved 9 February 2010 from `http://languagelog.ldc.upenn.edu/nll/`.

Mark Liberman. 2009b. No wug is too dax to be zonged. Retrieved 9 February 2010 from `http://languagelog.ldc.upenn.edu/nll/`.

Geoffrey K. Pullum. 2004. Too complex to avoid judgment? Retrieved 7 April 2010 from `http://itre.cis.upenn.edu/~myl/languagelog/`.

Evan Sandhaus. 2008. The New York Times Annotated Corpus. Linguistic Data Consortium, Philadelphia, PA.

Rion Snow, Brendan O'Connor, Daniel Jurafsky, and Andrew Y. Ng. 2008. Cheap and fast — But is it good? Evaluating non-expert annotations for natural language tasks. In *Proceedings of EMNLP-2008*, pages 254–263. Honolulu, HI.

John Trueswell and Michael J. Tanenhaus. 1994. Toward a lexicalist framework for constraint-based syntactic ambiguity resolution. In Charles Clifton, Lyn Frazier, and Keith Rayner, editors, *Perspectives on Sentence Processing*, pages 155–179. Lawrence Erlbaum, Hillsdale, NJ.

Peter Wason and Shuli Reich. 1979. A verbal illusion. *The Quarterly Journal of Experimental Psychology*, 31(4):591–597.

Theresa Wilson, Janyce Wiebe, and Paul Hoffmann. 2005. Recognizing contextual polarity in phrase-level sentiment analysis. In *Proceedings of HLT/EMNLP-2005*, pages 347–354. Vancouver, Canada.

Consonant Co-occurrence in Stems Across Languages: Automatic Analysis and Visualization of a Phonotactic Constraint

Thomas Mayer[1], **Christian Rohrdantz**[2], **Frans Plank**[1],
Peter Bak[2], **Miriam Butt**[1], **Daniel A. Keim**[2]
[1]Department of Linguistics, [2]Department of Computer Science
University of Konstanz, Germany
{thomas.mayer,christian.rohrdantz}@uni-konstanz.de

Abstract

In this paper, we explore the phenomenon of Similar Place Avoidance (SPA), according to which successive consonants within stems sharing the same place of articulation are avoided. This principle has recently been hypothesized as a universal tendency although evidence from only a few languages scattered across the world has been considered. Using methods taken from the field of Visual Analytics, which have demonstrably been shown to help with understanding complex interactions across large data sets, we investigated a large crosslinguistic lexical database (comprising data on more than 4,500 languages) and found that a universal tendency can indeed be maintained.

1 Introduction

Linguistic knowledge has traditionally been acquired by analyzing a manageable set of data, on the basis of which generalizations are posited that can then be tested on an extended set of data from the same language or comparative data from other languages. Tendencies, rather than absolute principles, are difficult to detect under this approach. This is true especially when they are obscured by counterexamples that happen to occur with high frequency, but that may be restricted to just a small minority of the overall pattern. This may prompt a researcher to discard a valid generalization from the outset. In recent years, a plethora of statistical and stochastic methods have therefore been pursued within linguistic research, leading to approaches such as stochastic Optimality Theory (Boersma and Hayes, 2001) or the use of statistics to detect crosslinguistic tendencies (Bickel, in press).

However, although the various statistical methods deal with data which exhibit very complex and often ill-understood interactions, analyses have not to date availed themselves of methodology currently being developed in the field of Visual Analytics, which allows us to use our powerful visual processing ability to understand and evaluate complex data sets (Keim et al., 2008; Thomas and Cook, 2005).

In this paper, we present an interdisciplinary effort whereby linguistically interesting patterns are automatically extracted, analyzed and visually presented so that an at-a-glance evaluation of linguistically significant patterns is made possible. In order to demonstrate that this technique is especially useful with phenomena that do not manifest themselves in absolute principles, but rather in statistical tendencies, we investigated a phenomenon that, on the basis of a comparatively sparse and unrepresentative data set, has recently been claimed to be a universal tendency (Pozdniakov and Segerer, 2007): *Similar Place Avoidance* (SPA). In this paper, we conduct a more representative study of about 4,500 languages. Our results allow an at-a-glance evaluation which shows that SPA indeed seems to be a valid language universal tendency.

Our work on SPA is part of a more widespread effort currently being conducted with respect to visually representing crosslinguistic sound patterns. In Rohrdantz et al. (2010), we already showed that phonological patterns in languages can be automatically extracted and visualized from corpora. Figure 1 displays the vowel harmony patterns that were extracted for Turkish in comparison with the lack of such patterns in a non-harmonic language like Spanish.

The remainder of this article is organized as follows. Section 2 introduces SPA. Section 3 provides an overview of the material that was used. A description of the calculations and statistical analyses is given in Section 4. Section 5 presents the results of the geo-spatial visualizations, partly

Proceedings of the 2010 Workshop on NLP and Linguistics: Finding the Common Ground, ACL 2010, pages 70–78,
Uppsala, Sweden, 16 July 2010.

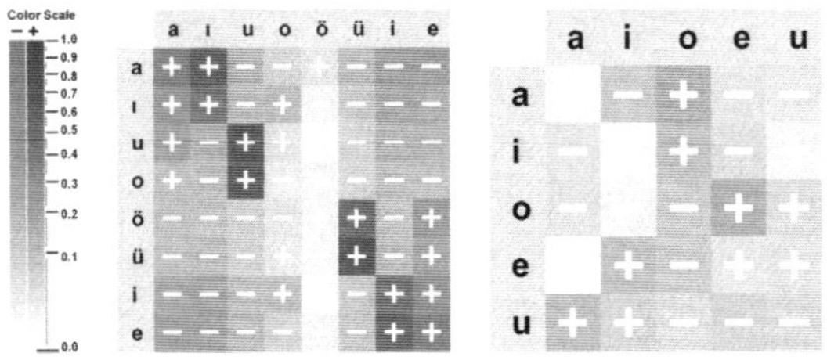

Figure 1: Turkish vowel harmony patterns (left). The matrix visualizaton was generated on the basis of the Turkish Bible text and shows the palatal (front/back) and labial (rounding) harmony blocks. Rows and columns are automatically sorted according to the similarity of vowels. For non-harmonic languages, such as Spanish (right), no such patterns can be detected.

with respect to a WALS map (Haspelmath et al., 2005). In the final section, we consider some implications of our findings and raise some questions for future research.

2 Similar Place Avoidance (SPA)

It has long been noted in studies on Semitic languages, especially Arabic, that there are constraints on the structure of triliteral consonant roots ($\sqrt{CCC}$) with respect to the phonological features of the individual consonants (Greenberg, 1950). The basic observation is that consonants with a similar place of articulation are avoided in non-derived forms. A similar observation has also been made with respect to the Proto-Indo-European (PIE) roots. Among other things, Iverson and Salmons (1992) note that Stop-V-Stop roots were very rare in PIE, representing only 3.5% of a lexicon of more than 2,000 items. Plank (1981:221f) observes that Modern German tends to avoid verbal stems with identical consonants in initial and final positions (allowing for differences in voicing), and that those verbs with identical initial and final consonants which do exist are all morphologically regular. This indicates that they are not basic verbs, but represent a technique of word formation, perhaps derivative of reduplication as especially common in child or child-directed language.[1]

[1]Note that the early speech of children is characterized by the opposite effect of SPA: both consonants and vowels tend to share the same place of articulation (Fikkert and Levelt, 2010), with greater and greater differentiation being achieved in the course of language acquisition. The reasons for this remain to be investigated.

Looking at suprasegmental features, Leben (1973) argued that a similar restriction holds for the co-occurrence of tones in underlying representations. In the framework of Autosegmental Phonology this has become known as the *Obligatory Contour Principle* (OCP), which precludes sequences of identical tones from underlying representations. This principle has since been understood more generally as a prohibition on similar items and has thus also been used in relation with the SPA bias in Semitic radicals.

More recently, the application of SPA with respect to stem-internal consonants has been claimed for other non-Semitic languages as well. Pozdniakov and Segerer (2007) found impressive support for it in their sample of Atlantic and Bantu languages of Niger-Congo and further tested its crosslinguistic validity for some more languages or language groups (Mande, Kwa, Ubangi, Sara-Bongo-Bagirmi, Chadic, Malagasy, Indo-European, Nostratic, Mongolian, Basque, Quechua, Kamilaroi, Port Moresby Pidgin English) with similar results. Table 1 shows their findings across all 31 languages in their sample. It can be seen that the highest negative numbers are in the main diagonal of the matrix, which is exactly what SPA would predict.

	P	T	C	K
P	−15	+11	+5	−5
T	+12	−10	−5	+13
C	+8	−5	−6	+8
K	−3	+8	+5	−15

Table 1: Results in Pozdniakov and Segerer (2007). The numbers indicate the overall sum of cells with negative vs. positive values with regard to successions of places of articulation (see Section 3 for a description of the labels *P, T, C* and *K*) for all languages in their sample. Positive and negative values have been assigned if the observed absolute value was at least 15% above (respectively below) the expected value. Compare their results with the left matrix in Figure 3.

3 Database and methodology

The data that underlies all the subsequent work presented in this paper have been taken from the Automated Similarity Judgment Program (ASJP; Wichmann et al., 2010), which aims at achieving a computerized lexicostatistical analysis of the world's languages. To this end, Wichmann and his collaborators have collected Swadesh list items for over 4,500 languages. The so-called Swadesh list was developed by Morris Swadesh in the 1940–50s with the aim of having a basic set of vocabulary items which are culturally neutral and which one would expect to be stable over time. The original idea of a Swadesh list was to be able to compare and test languages with respect to genealogical relations.

The Swadesh items in the Wichmann et al. database are transcribed in the ASJP orthography, which uses standard ASCII characters to encode the sounds of the world's languages, but does merge some of the distinctions made by the IPA. Furthermore, stress, tone and vowel length are not recorded in the database. However, for the purpose of our investigation the transcription is suitable because place of articulation is sufficiently distinguished.

We decided to experiment with two different approaches for dividing up the place of articulation features. One approach (PTCK) is based on the arrangement in Pozdniakov and Segerer (2007) and distinguishes four places of articulation for labial (*P*), dental (and alveolar) (*T*), (alveo-)palatal (*C*) and velar (*K*) consonants. A second grouping (LCD) only distinguishes three places of articulation: labial (*L*), coronal (*C*) and dorsal (*D*).[2] According to this classification the consonants of all the items in the database can be assigned to one of these symbols, as shown in Table 2.

LCD	PTCK	ASJP	IPA
L	*P*	p, b, m, f, v, w	p, ɸ, b, β, m, f, v, w
C	*T*	8, 4, t, d, s, z, c, n, S, Z	θ, ð, n̪, t, d, s, z, ts, dz, n, ʃ, ʒ
	C	C, j, T, l, L, r, y	ʧ, ʤ, c, ɟ, l, ʎ, ɭ, ʎ, r, ɾ, j
D	*K*	5, k, g, x, N, q, G, X, 7, h	ɲ, k, ɡ, x, ɣ, ŋ, q, ɣ, χ, ʁ, ħ, ʕ, ʔ, h, ɦ,

Table 2: Assignment of consonants to symbols. All varieties of "click"-sounds have been ignored.

Experiments with using the four-way distinction vs. the three-way distinction showed that *T* and *C* in the four-way grouping behave very similarly with respect to the transitions to other places of articulation (see Section 4.2). We therefore decided to use the three-way distinction for the bulk of our calculations and visualizations and only sporadically resort to the four-way grouping when a more fine-grained distinction is needed.

Furthermore, we decided to only include those cases where the first and second consonants are preceded (or followed, respectively) by another vowel or a word boundary and are therefore not part of a consonant cluster. We mainly did this in order to minimize the noise caused by consonants of inflectional markers that tend to assimilate in such clusters.

In the literature on root morphemes in Semitic, it has been noted that the consonants within triliteral radicals behave differently with respect to OCP. Greenberg (1950:162) remarks that while the first and second consonants are usually not identical, the same does not hold for the second and third consonants, which frequently constitute the well-known geminate subtype of Semitic verbs. However, for our work we understand OCP as it was later formulated within the framework of autosegmental phonology (Leben, 1973; McCarthy, 1986; Goldsmith, 1976) in that adjacent identical elements (here in the sense of identical with respect to place of articulation) are prohibited, under the assumption that consonants are adjacent to each other (on the C tier) even when they are separated by vowels in the linear sequence of phonemes within the word.

For the purposes of our experiment, we considered the relevant context for adjacency to be one where consonants are separated by exactly one vowel.[3] Note that since the basis for our calculations were not stems in the language but the citation forms that are used in the Swadesh lists, we also get noise from inflectional markers that are attached to these forms and might have the same place of articulation irrespective of the stem to which they attach.[4]

Finally, there are several shortcomings of the

[2] Radical and laryngeal, which are commonly employed in the phonological literature as yet another place distinction, are subsumed under dorsal.

[3] Since vowel length is not marked in the ASJP database, long vowels are also included.

[4] Assimilation processes are far more frequent than dissimilation processes in this context so that it is more likely that the same place of articulation features are to be expected when an inflectional marker is present.

material in the database with respect to our investigation which must be kept in mind. OCP/SPA has been claimed to apply with respect to underlying or non-derived representations. Previous work has been done on the basis of stem (or root) lists. Depending on the language, Swadesh list items are not always stems, but whole words in their citation forms. For instance, while both English and German use the infinitive as the citation form for verbal stems, in English the infinitive is identical to the stem whereas in German it is marked with the suffix *-en*. In other languages, verbs can also be cited by inflected forms other than the infinitive (e.g., the 3rd person singular perfective in Arabic, or the first person singular indicative present in Latin). The same holds for nouns or other word classes that are included in the Swadesh list. Another problematic aspect is the fact that it also contains items (such as personal pronouns) that are not lexical in the strict sense of the meaning and are realized as bound forms in many languages.

Apart from that, the number of items for each language in the ASJP database varied greatly from only a few to one hundred. Moreover, the number of CVC sequences within the items differed greatly from one language to another, depending on the phonotactic properties of the languages. Previous statistical studies have relied on a much larger number of stems and consonant sequences. Pozdniakov and Segerer's (2007) statistics, for example, were calculated on the basis of 495 to 17,944 CVC successions for the languages in their sample.[5] In contrast, our statistics are based on much fewer CVC successions, ranging from 21 to 246 per language. Nevertheless, our results actually correspond to the main findings of their study so that we think that the data are good enough for our purposes.

4 Automated statistical analysis

4.1 Methodology

In a first step, for each language in the sample an elementary statistical processing is performed. Thereby, all successions of places of articulation occurring in the Swadesh list items are identified and counted. To do so, we define a succession of places of articulation as a binary sequence of consonants (C-C). These consonants have to appear within a word and have to be separated by exactly one vowel (V). Before and after the succession either word boundaries (#) or vowels have to appear. Hence, the following regular expression is used to extract C-C successions (marked in bold): $[\#|V]\mathbf{C}V\mathbf{C}[\#|V]$. Next, each consonant is assigned to one of the three major articulation place categories *labial*, *coronal* and *dorsal*. The succession counts are summarized in a quadratic matrix where the rows represent the preceding place of articulation and the columns the following place of articulation. Each matrix cell contains the number of times the respective place of articulation succession could be observed in the corpus. Subsequently, for each of the 9 possible successions a contingency table was created (Table 3).

	P_2	$\neg P_2$
P_1	$A: n(P_1 \rightarrow P_2)$	$B: n(P_1 \rightarrow \neg P_2)$
$\neg P_1$	$C: n(\neg P_1 \rightarrow P_2)$	$D: n(\neg P_1 \rightarrow \neg P_2)$

Table 3: Contingency table for the articulation place (P) succession from P_1 to P_2.

The succession counts were used to calculate ϕ coefficients, where A, B, C and D correspond to the four cells in Table 3.

$$\phi = \sqrt{\frac{\chi^2}{(A+B+C+D)}} \qquad (1)$$

The ϕ coefficient is a measure for the degree of association between two variables which can be derived from the fourfold χ^2 statistical significance test (see Rummel, 1970:298f for details). Sample ϕ values for the place of articulation successions of Egyptian Arabic can be seen in Table 4. A visual representation of the same matrix is provided in Figure 2. Note the at-a-glance analysis made possible by Figure 2 vs. Table 4.

	labial	coronal	dorsal
labial	−0.360	+0.187	+0.183
coronal	+0.259	−0.243	−0.068
dorsal	−0.010	+0.097	−0.121

Table 4: Matrix of ϕ values for Egyptian Arabic.

Figure 2 shows an example in which all diagonal values (self-successions of places of articulation) have negative associations. This tendency

[5] Note that they also included cases where the first and second consonant are part of a consonant cluster, which we ignored for our calculations. Furthermore, those languages where the number of consonant successions in the data was 20 or below were not included in our visualizations, thereby reducing the number of languages from about 4,500 to 3,200.

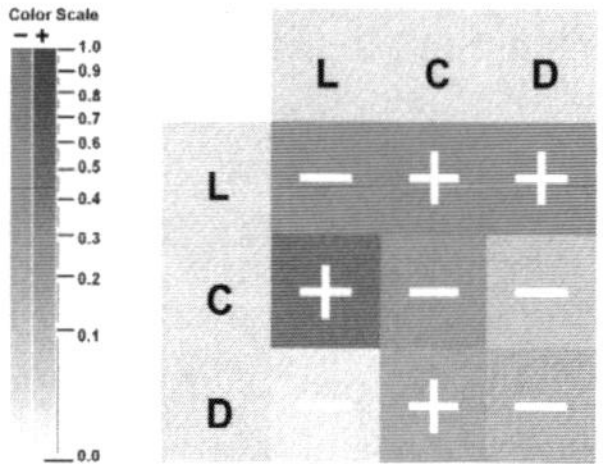

Figure 2: Visualization of the ϕ matrix from Table 4 (Egyptian Arabic), *L* stands for labial, *C* for coronal and *D* for dorsal. It can be seen that all diagonal values (successions of the same place of articulation) have negative associations (red color).

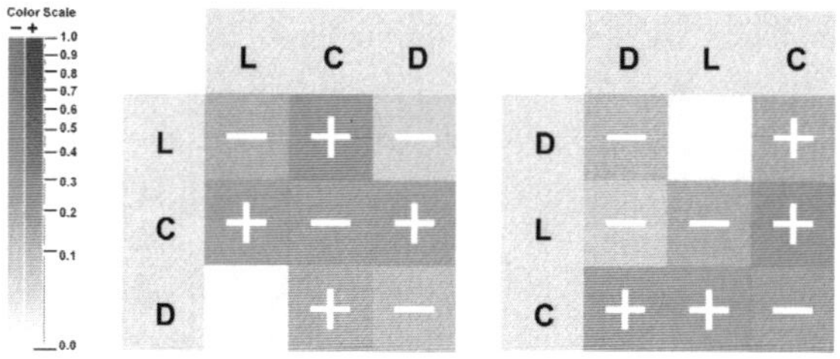

Figure 4: The ϕ matrix considering only the three main categories for all the data across languages. In the left figure, the categories are sorted according to their position in the oral cavity. In the right figure, the categories are sorted automatically, which shows that *D* and *L* are more similar to each other than *D* and *C*.

to alternate places of articulation can be observed in most languages and in the overall matrix visualizations including all data from all languages in the database (Figure 4).

4.2 General relations among places of articulation

As already mentioned, we tested whether it is useful to distinguish the two different subcategories dental (and alveolar) (*T*), and (alveo-)palatal (*C*). Figure 3 shows the resulting association values ϕ of place successions.

It can clearly be seen that *T* and *C* behave very similarly. A further interesting observation is that places of articulation tend to alternate (negative diagonal values for self-successions). As revealed in the succession graph of Figure 3, the places of articulation do not remain the same, but change to the closest alternative(s). In the case of *P* and *K* the closest distinct places of articulation (*T* and *C*) are preferred. In the case of *T* and *C*, however, this is somewhat different. Apparently, direct alternations between both are less probable. One plausible explanation could be that they are not distinct enough and thus either *K* or *P* are preferred as a following place of articulation, both having roughly the same distance. These observations led us to merge the places *T* and *C* in our further analyses and distinguish labial, coronal and dorsal consonants only, as in Figure 4.

Note that the cross pattern on the left in Figure 4, which now emerges very clearly, reinforces the hypothesis that the closest distinct place of articulation is preferred as successor.

4.3 Distribution across languages

Next, we examined the distribution of ϕ values for self-successions of places of articulation in about 3,200 languages. Self-successions correspond to the diagonal values of the ϕ matrices from the upper left to the lower right. As can be seen in the histogram in Figure 6, the peak of the distribution is clearly located in the area of negative association values. In the box-plots of Figure 5, which show the distributions for all three places of articulation separately, it is clearly visible that for each of the three places of articulation at least 75% of the languages included show negative associations. Furthermore, it can be seen that most outliers disappear when taking only the languages for which most data is available and thus statistics are more reliable. The same can be seen in the scatter plot in Figure 6, where the average ϕ value is always negative if the number of successions exceeds a certain threshold. For all three categories, the figures demonstrate that the same place of articulation is generally less frequently maintained than expected if there were no interdependencies between consonant co-occurrences.

5 Visualization of geo-spatial patterns

The most common approach to visually represent crosslinguistic information on areal (or genealogical) patterns is to put each language as a single pixel or a small icon to its location on a map. For instance, the WALS database (Haspelmath et al., 2005) includes 141 maps on diverse structural (phonological, grammatical, lexical) properties of languages. We transformed the results of our SPA statistics for each language in the ASJP database

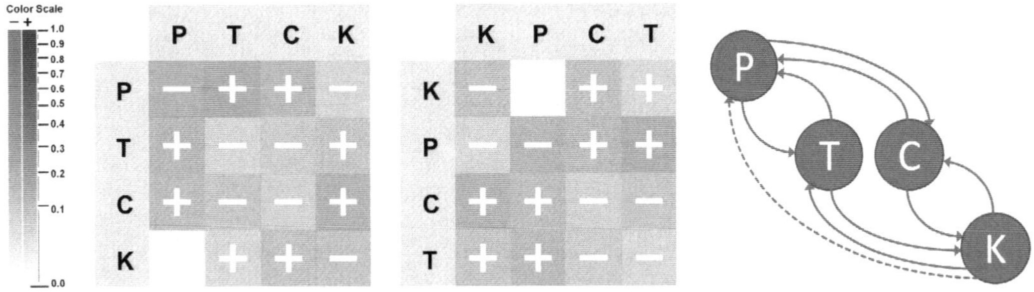

Figure 3: Successions of *P*, *T*, *C* and *K* in all languages. The "+" and "−" signs indicate the polarity of a succession (going from row to column category). The color saturation of the background indicates the strength of association. In the left figure, places of articulation are sorted according to their position in the oral cavity, in the middle figure an automatic similarity sorting of matrix rows and columns was applied. The right part of the figure shows an alternative view only on those successions that have a positive association.

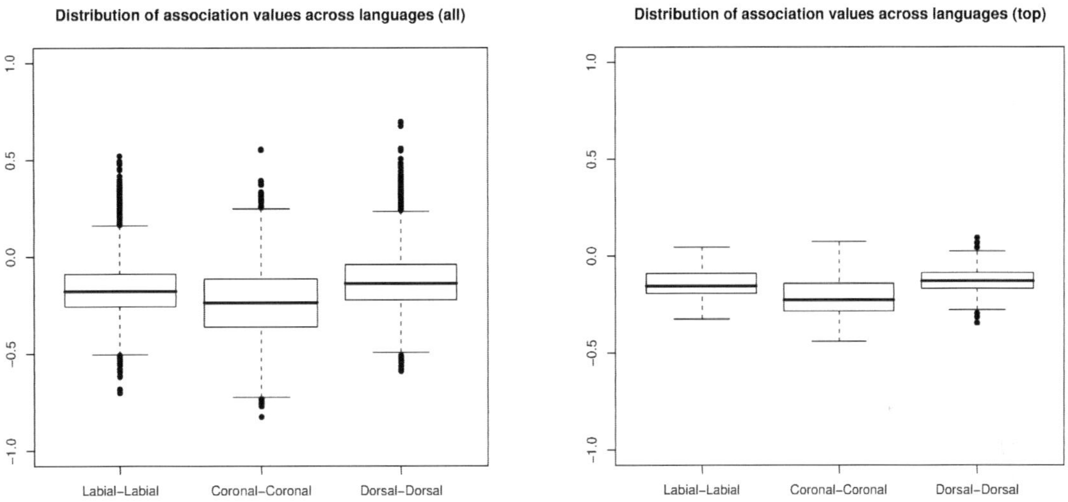

Figure 5: Boxplots showing the distribution of association strength values (ϕ) for self-successions of places of articulation. For the left boxplots about 3,200 languages were considered for which the Swadesh lists contained more than 20 successions. For the right boxplots only the top 99 languages were considered for which the Swadesh lists contained at least 100 successions, thereby removing most outliers and reducing the variance.

that is also included in the WALS database into a WALS map (Figure 7). The matrix visualization has been simplified in that the color of the icon represents the number of cells in the diagonal of the matrix whose value was below zero, i.e., the higher the number (0-3) the better the language conforms to SPA.

Some of the drawbacks of these maps include a high degree of overlap of data points in densely populated areas and the lack of correlation between information content and area size. In Figure 7, the fact that those languages with fewer negative diagonal cells are plotted on top of those with a higher number slightly distorts the overall picture that most languages adhere to the principle.[6] Besides that, the overall pattern in the densely populated areas is hardly visible, while sparsely populated areas waste space and hide the informational

[6]Likewise, the visualization would suggest to much adherence to the principle if those languages with more negative diagonal cells were plotted on top of those with fewer negative cells.

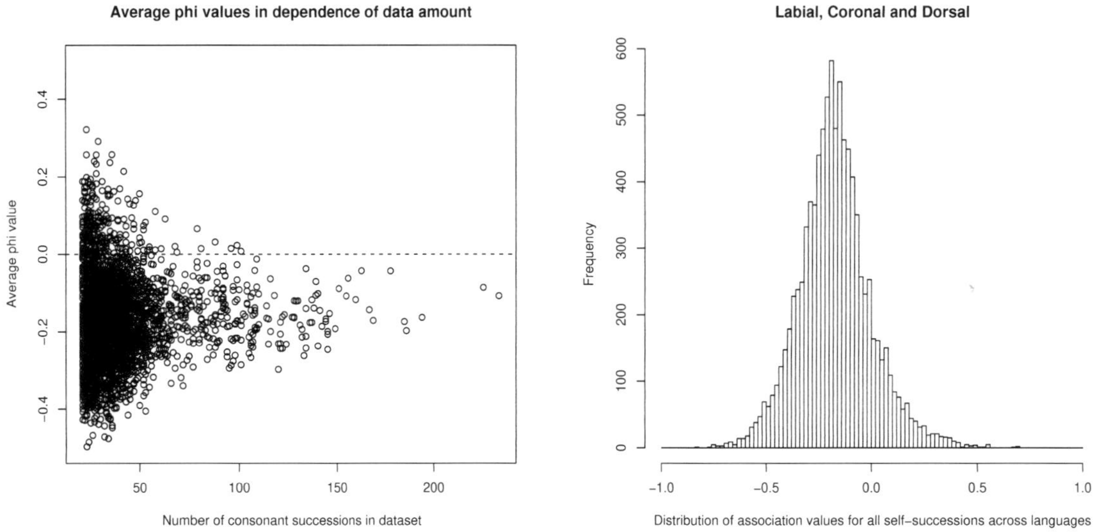

Figure 6: The scatter plot on the left displays the average ϕ values for self-successions of all places of articulation depending on the number of consonant successions (CVC) for each language in the sample. The histogram on the right shows the distribution of association strength values (ϕ) for self-successions of places of articulation in more than 3200 languages.

details. Finally, small clusters are difficult to find — they are not noticeable, and are sometimes even obscured by large clusters.

In order to avoid overlapping pixels we used a circular arrangement around the original location in the current analysis, taking the given ordering of elements into account (Bak et al., 2009a). The ordering usually corresponds to the coloring attribute starting with colors that occur least frequently. With this arrangement a natural looking visualization without artifacts is generated.

A way to obtain more space for regions with a high point density are Cartograms, which distort regions such that their size corresponds to a statistical attribute (Bak et al., 2009b; Tobler, 2004), in this case the number of languages in the database. The advantage is that more space is reserved to plot all important information on the map. In Figure 8, we show the density equalized distortion by cartograms and the overlap-free representation of the data points using pixel placement. Neighborhood relations and region shapes are at the same time maintained as accurately as possible in order to guarantee recognizability despite of distortion. The visualization reveals several clusters of non-conforming languages (marked with boxes). It remains for future work to investigate whether these clusters are an artifact of the database that we used or if they manifest an areal feature. Figure 8, in contrast to Figure 7, shows the 3,200 languages we investigated more closely and not just the ones included in WALS.

The representation thereby enables investigating spatial patterns free of hidden data and distributional biases.

6 Conclusions and future work

Our crosslinguistic investigation of SPA has confirmed the hypothesis that the phenomenon of Similar Place Avoidance is not a particular trait of Semitic languages, for which it was previously described, but is a linguistic universal tendency which can be observed in languages which are both genealogically and geographically unrelated. This can clearly be seen in the visualizations that display the conformity of each language in the database with respect to SPA. The overall picture for all languages not only shows that successive consonants with the same place of articulation tend to be avoided, but also that there is a tendency to avoid places of articulation that are too far away from the preceding place (cf. Figures 3 and 4).

We combine methods from statistics, NLP and Visual Analytics to provide a novel way of automatically assessing and visualizing linguistic features across a wide range of languages, thus al-

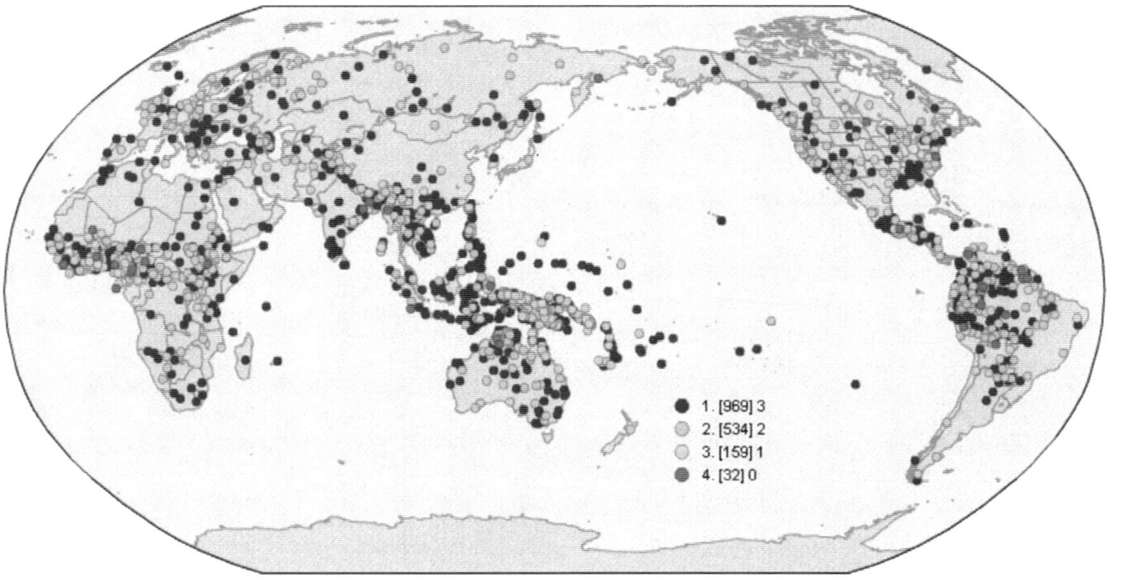

Figure 7: WALS map of the languages and their behavior with respect to SPA. The color indicates the number of self-succession ϕ values which are negative, i.e., which adhere to the SPA principle. Color mapping is from blue (conforming to SPA) to red. The numbers in square brackets indicate the number of languages in this group.

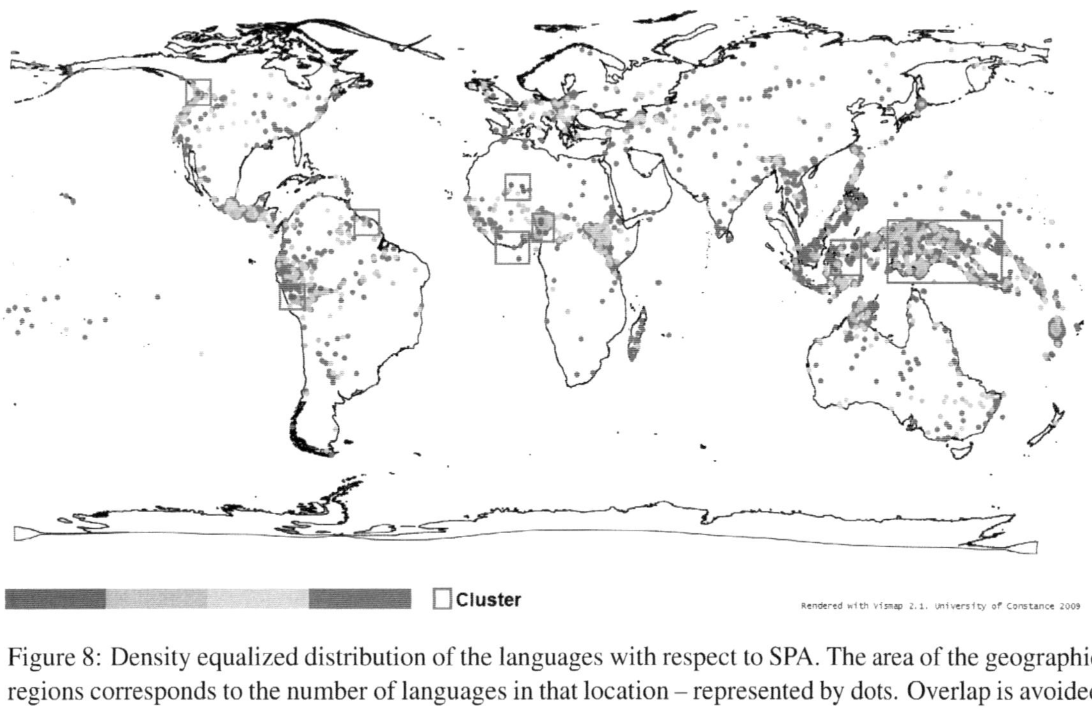

Figure 8: Density equalized distribution of the languages with respect to SPA. The area of the geographic regions corresponds to the number of languages in that location – represented by dots. Overlap is avoided using pixel-placement. The color mapping corresponds to the one used in the WALS map (Figure 7). Locations of nonconforming languages are highlighted with red boxes. Note that the number of languages in this map is about twice the number in the WALS map (7).

lowing for a gain of new insights and raising further interesting research questions that otherwise might easily go unrecognized.

With respect to SPA a more detailed exploration of the intricacies of phonological interdepencies is needed as part of our more widespread study of visually representing sound patterns in languages. As already hinted at in Pozdniakov and Segerer (2007), there are various other fascinating phenomena that are worth looking at, especially in regard to the interaction of vowels and consonants or vowel dependencies (such as vowel harmony) and consonant dependencies (such as SPA or consonant harmony). In particular, one could investigate why some languages apparently do not conform to SPA and if there is any co-variation to be uncovered between the adherence to the principle and other factors that might be interesting to explore and possibly reveal new insights into the structure of languages.

Acknowledgments

This work has been funded by the research initiative "Computational Analysis of Linguistic Development" at the University of Konstanz. The authors would like to thank Aditi Lahiri and two anonymous reviewers for valuable comments and suggestions.

References

Peter Bak, Florian Mansmann, Halldor Janetzko, and Daniel Keim. 2009a. Spatiotemporal analysis of sensor logs using growth ring maps. *IEEE Transactions on Visualization and Computer Graphics*, 15(6):913–920.

Peter Bak, Matthias Schaefer, Andreas Stoffel, Daniel Keim, and Itzhak Omer. 2009b. Density equalizing distortion of large geographic point sets. *Journal of Cartographic and Geographic Information Science (CaGIS)*, 36(3):237–250.

Balthasar Bickel. in press. Absolute and statistical universals. In Patrick C. Hogan, editor, *The Cambridge Encyclopedia of the Language Sciences*. Cambridge: Cambridge University Press.

Paul Boersma and Bruce Hayes. 2001. Empirical tests of the gradual learning algorithm. *Linguistic Inquiry*, 32:45–86.

Paula Fikkert and Clara C. Levelt. 2010. How does place fall into place? The lexicon and emergent constraints in the developing phonological grammar. In Peter Avery, B. Elan Dresher, and Keren Rice, editors, *Contrast in Phonology: Perception and Acquisition*. Berlin: Mouton de Gruyter.

John Goldsmith. 1976. *Autosegmental phonology*. Ph.D. thesis, Massachusetts Institute of Technology.

Joseph H. Greenberg. 1950. The patterning of root morphemes in Semitic. *Word*, 6:161–182.

Martin Haspelmath, Matthew S. Dryer, David Gil, and Bernard Comrie. 2005. The World Atlas of Language Structures Online. URL: http://wals.info/.

Gregory K. Iverson and Joseph C. Salmonts. 1992. The phonology of the Proto-Indo-European root structure constraint. *Lingua*, 87:293–320.

Daniel A. Keim, Florian Mansmann, Joern Schneidewind, Jim Thomas, and Hartmut Ziegler. 2008. Visual analytics: Scope and challenges. In *Visual Data Mining: Theory, Techniques and Tools for Visual Analytics*, Lecture Notes in Computer Science, pages 76–91. Springer.

Wiliam R. Leben. 1973. *Suprasegmental phonology*. Ph.D. thesis, Massachusetts Institute of Technology.

John J. McCarthy. 1986. OCP effects: Gemination and antigemination. *Linguistic Inquiry*, 17:207–263.

Frans Plank. 1981. *Morphologische (Ir-)Regularitäten: Aspekte der Wortstrukturtheorie*. Tübingen: Gunter Narr Verlag.

Konstantin Pozdniakov and Guillaume Segerer. 2007. Similar Place Avoidance: A statistical universal. *Linguistic Typology*, 11(2):307–348.

Christian Rohrdantz, Thomas Mayer, Miriam Butt, Frans Plank, and Daniel A. Keim. 2010. Comparative visual analysis of cross-linguistic features. In *Proceedings of the International Symposium on Visual Analytics Science and Technology (EuroVAST 2010)*, pages 27–32.

Rudolph J. Rummel. 1970. *Applied Factor Analysis*. Evanston, IL: Nortwestern University Press.

James J. Thomas and Kristin A. Cook. 2005. *Illuminating the Path: The Research and Development Agenda for Visual Analytics*. National Visualization and Analytics Ctr.

Waldo Tobler. 2004. Thirty five years of computer cartograms. *Association of American Geographer*, 94(1):58–73.

Injecting Linguistics into NLP through Annotation

Eduard Hovy
USC/ISI
4676 Admiralty Way
Marina del Rey, CA 90292
USA
hovy@isi.edu

Over the past 20 years, the size of the *L* in Computational Linguistics has been shrinking relative to the size of the *C*. The result is that we are increasingly becoming a community of uninformed but sophisticated engineers, applying to problems very complex machine learning techniques that use very simple (simplistic?) analyses/theories. (Try finding a theoretical account of subjectivity, opinion, entailment, or inference in publications surrounding the associated competitions of the past few years.)

When we grow tired of embarrassing ourselves, what should we do? Fortunately, injecting some linguistic (and other) sophistication into our work is not that complicated. The key is annotation: by using a theoretically informed set of choices rather than a bottom-up naive one, we can have annotators tag corpora with labels that reflect some underlying theories. While the large-C contingent of our community will not care, researchers interested in investigating language rather than processing will be able to find new ways to connect with Corpus Linguists, Psycholinguists, and even Ontologists.

It turns out that many of our surrounding academic communities – Linguists, Political Scientists, Biocurators, etc. – have been performing annotation for years in order to build and prove their theories. They have however been largely unaware of the power of NLP technology and the benefits we can bring to them. There is a natural marriage – several, actually – waiting to happen.

What is the benefit to us? What's wrong with simply continuing to use half-baked annotation schemes to train our machine learning systems on? Several things:

- half-baked schemes generally fail in the long run-that's why more-sophisticated ones are developed
- there are dozens to hundreds of graduate students and young researchers in surrounding communities eager to help build corpora by running annotation efforts and using the problems uncovered while annotating to drive further theory formation
- because they're generally more 'correct', more-sophisticated annotations allow stacking of multiple phenomena upon the same material with fewer internal inconsistencies and problems.

Such stacking eventually enables multi-phenomenon analysis and mutual disambiguation in ways that an incommensurately annotated corpus does not.

Proceedings of the 2010 Workshop on NLP and Linguistics: Finding the Common Ground, ACL 2010, page 79,
Uppsala, Sweden, 16 July 2010. ©2010 Association for Computational Linguistics

Author Index